PROFESSIONAL LEADERSHIP IN SCHOOLS

effective middle management & subject leadership

james williams

KOGAN

Dedication

This book is dedicated to my wife, Joan, for her understanding, critical comment and the loss of many weekends during its writing. It is also for my late father, Ralph Williams, from whom I inherited the attributes that all managers need – patience, authority and, above all, respect for others.

For whom I have managed and been managed by, thank you for your unacknowledged contributions.

First published in 2002

Kogan Page Limited
120 Pentonville Road
London N1 9JN
UK

Stylus Publishing Inc
22883 Quicksilver Drive
Sterling VA 20166-2012
USA

© James Williams, 2002

British Library Cataloguing in Publication Data

A CIP record for this book is available from the British Library.

ISBN 0 7494 3292 6

Typeset by JS Typesetting, Wellingborough, Northants
Printed and bound in Great Britain by Clays Ltd, St Ives plc

CONTENTS

Introduction   *iv*

1 What is management?   1
2 Leadership and decision making   17
3 Time management   29
4 Developing action plans   41
5 Team building and motivating   50
6 Effective communication   66
7 Managing meetings   79
8 The role of the mentor   86
9 Managing staff performance   96
10 Staff selection and interviewing   104
11 Managing change and dealing with conflict   118
12 Legal aspects of running a department   128
13 Financial management   140

Appendix A   *150*

Appendix B   *152*

References and bibliography   *155*

Index   *162*

INTRODUCTION

The Gordon Gekko (*Wall Street*, 1987) film image of a hard-nosed, 'lunch is for wimps' tycoon who is the personification of strong management will, sadly, exist somewhere in the real world. This image is summed up by a line from the film, spoken by Gekko, *'Well, in my book, you either do it right, or you get eliminated!'* This image, this attitude, has no place in the effective management of schools. Management is about people. It is not about results, resources or retribution. Models of management exist in all walks of life and our thinking as managers is sometimes shaped by images that may only exist in the minds of Hollywood film makers. This book seeks to overturn this hard-nosed image and present instead strategies and practices that lead to effective management.

This is not to say that strong management cannot, and should not, be in place. Unfortunately, far too often it is confused with the aggressive, uncompromising stance of the bully. Strong, firm management can be achieved without regularly reducing staff to tears or building resentment, even fear. It can be achieved with clarity of thought and vision, with firm guidance and leadership directing the department towards achieving a common goal. Strong means clarity of communication with flexibility to change and adjust where the need arises. Strong means dedicated, dedicated to achieving raised standards of learning and teaching.

WHAT IS THIS BOOK ABOUT?

This book is about effective management. That means strong management, firm management, successful management. The book has arisen from my desire to see managers in schools attain high standards of professional competence without resorting to crisis management. The essence of management theory is what actually works in practice, not what looks good on paper. The underlying philosophy of the book is one that recognizes that people need two things in order to lead and to be led successfully: they need motivation and they need good working conditions. This is summed up by Herzberg's motivation-hygiene theory. Simply throwing money at people will not, in the long term, motivate them and allow them to achieve. A delicate balance has to be set between financial reward, personal reward and conditions of service. In the short term, the government has met demands for increased motivation and job satisfaction in teaching with short-term pay deals and financial motivators such as the notion of crossing thresholds for extra financial gain. They have heralded this as the key to motivating graduates to become teachers and as the solution to retaining the swathes of dedicated teachers leaving the profession. The government attaches strings to this, related to performance, and the jury is still out on whether or not it has addressed the fundamental problem of teacher recruitment and retention. But the focus in schools and for the profession has now turned to conditions of service. Many teachers have stated quite openly that in lieu of more money, more time would be a greater motivator and lead to greater retention. This is especially true for the mature career-orientated teacher. There is a ladder of promotion in schools that can be climbed by those who wish a greater financial reward, culminating in the rewards payable to the leadership group and to headteachers. Arguments abound about whether the actual payments for both main scale teachers and leadership group teachers are high enough or closely enough linked to performance, but there is a unanimous voice that cries out for a reduction in workload and better working conditions. This voice is beginning to be heard and needs to be taken notice of. In the case of Scotland, the voice has resulted in action. In a groundbreaking pay deal, teachers were offered a substantial pay rise, in excess of 20 per cent phased in over a three-year period and, more importantly, a limit on the amount of contact time and a nominal 35-hour week with moves towards a nominal 22.5 hours of contact time. This begins to address the motivation side of Herzberg's theory, with pay that begins to approach a level that is commensurate with the professional nature of teaching. It also begins to address the hygiene side of the theory, attacking the working conditions with nominal limitations on contact hours and the length of the working week.

WHO IS THIS BOOK AIMED AT?

The book is aimed at teachers who are newly appointed heads of department, those aspiring to be heads of department, or experienced heads of department that need practical help and advice on new situations. The book will also be of use to those who are studying for a professional diploma or higher degree in education management. It is also a useful primer for those considering fast-track promotion or entry on to the national professional qualification for headteachers (NPQH).

With the recent changes in management structures in schools and the development of the new leadership group, there is a recognition that management in schools requires more than just experience as a teacher. The new National College for Leadership is primarily aimed at headteachers and is charged with improving the management skills of that group and of the leadership group in general. It is clear that a skilled headteacher is needed to lift a failing school from spiralling down to special measures and reverse that spiral to achieve good standards of teaching and learning for all its pupils. The College does not provide the same for middle managers. Yet it is true to say that what makes a good school a great school and what lifts a failing school from the depths is not just the work and vision of the headteacher alone. A brilliant headteacher, without the right middle management layer, will almost certainly fail. The recent high-profile creation of so-called 'superheads' also resulted in some spectacular failures on their part. It would be wrong to say that this was the result of a poor middle management, but well-appointed strong middle managers will have a considerable effect on the chances of success of a fresh start for a failing school. For good schools, maintenance of their position in the league tables or, more importantly, their position in the hearts and minds of the parents and pupils can only be achieved with a strong effective layer of middle management. This is recognized in the TTA (Teacher Training Agency) and the consequent publication of their National Standards for Subject Leaders. The book is also rooted in this belief and, therefore, in those same standards.

WHAT DOES THIS BOOK OFFER?

What this book offers is practical, pragmatic advice about how management in schools can be effected that also considers the motivational needs of staff and the need to raise performance. It offers strategies for motivation and team building (Chapter 5) and time management (Chapter 3). This is not a book of management tips and one-liners; it isn't a '60-minute departmental manager' book. It has, underlying all of the strategies described, a theoretical framework and therefore links theory, practice and results. Many of the strategies come from personal experience of running a large department and others from helping existing managers create a management style for themselves that is fit for the purpose. As an evolutionary palaeontologist at heart, I am intimately aware of the notion of 'survival of the fittest'. This phrase has been used and abused by many in an attempt to justify a hard-nosed approach to management. Those who use it for this purpose are deluded. A common misconception is that evolution, as a process, is about ever-increasing complexity and that fitness equates to strength. Both of these notions are incorrect. Being fit for the purpose can in many instances mean that simplicity wins the day and that physical strength may be a disadvantage. The more complex an organism is, the more it requires in the way of energy and resources in order to let it run at maximum efficiency. Simple organisms require less. This is analogous to businesses, and to schools. Large, strong businesses require vast resources in order to keep them running. Small, simple organizations can be better suited to their environment and perform just as efficiently and just as well on fewer resources and less complexity. There lies, between the smallest, simplest organization and the largest, most complex one, a happy medium. Good schools, effective schools, achieve that happy medium.

WHERE DID THE BOOK ORIGINATE?

The book originated from a TTA-sponsored course on effective middle management written and presented by myself from Brunel University. The course was aimed at Master's level and successful completion of the course and the production of either a portfolio or work or an assignment on an aspect of management gained M-level credits. The course has been successfully run at three schools and as a four-day intensive management course. In addition, a reduced version of the course was also successfully produced for commercial INSET on offer around the country. In its first year the course was inspected by OFSTED and gained praise for its practical approach, underpinned by sound theory. The advice, help and theory contained within the following 13 chapters work, and many heads of department and aspiring heads have put into operation aspects of the skills presented. Many teachers who attended the courses have now secured posts as heads of department and seconds, and this is a testament to the overriding principle of the book: what works, and not just what looks good on paper.

HOW SHOULD THIS BOOK BE USED?

Each chapter of the book will be a self-contained view of a specific aspect of management. The book can be read from start to finish and will act as a useful theoretical and practical guide to management for those who are studying for a professional qualification in management or for an academic qualification such as a Master's degree. As a manager you will meet many situations over a period of time and this book can act as a guide. As each chapter is self-contained, you may dip into and out of the book at specific times, say when a work-related incident presents itself and you require instant help and advice. If you are a new manager, with little management experience, then you will want to look at what management means (Chapter 1) and what the various management styles are that you may need to employ. As a manager you will also be a leader and it is easy to confuse leadership and management, so you need to be clear about the difference between them. Chapter 2 clarifies this position.

The issue of time management is of crucial importance if you are, as a manager, to be an effective worker. Chapter 3 sets out how to identify where your time is currently being used (efficiently and inefficiently) and describes strategies for managing your time more effectively. Action planning is an integral part of school management and each year many work hours are devoted to action plans that merely pay lip service to the whole school development plan. Chapter 4 describes a more effective way of constructing and effecting action plans that do not just sit as extra paper in the departmental handbook. Whether or not you are new to management, the issue of team building and motivation is crucial to successful management and leadership of a department. New managers may have to shape an existing team and existing managers will have to continually reassess the team and induct new members as staff movement and changes take place. Knowing the phases that teams go through will help both to reassure and to encourage new and existing managers to persevere with change and implement new working practises. The storming phase (pp 56–57) is the most disconcerting one. It is useful to know that it is just a phase and, like the sleepless nights all new parents experience, it will end and future growth will take place.

The essential skill that every manager and leader must have is that of communication. Interestingly, teachers are, by the nature of their job, supposed to be effective communicators. So why, when it comes to communication to our peers, our line managers and with our staff, do these essential skills seem to desert so many? While the book cannot answer this question, Chapter 6 provides a synthesis of what good communication is about and how to learn the skills. At no point will the skills of effective communication be more necessary than in meetings. The notion of meetings is, for many, anathema to good management. Weak managers are often characterized by their inability to chair effective meetings. In truth, much time is wasted by unnecessary meetings. This is best illustrated by the number of times that meetings turn into moaning sessions. The result is demotivated staff, resentful of the time wasted. Managing a good meeting is an art and the art is clearly explained in Chapter 7.

With performance management set to become an integral part of the job of managers in schools, there are a number of issues that require careful, sensitive handling. These encompass:

❑ staff selection and interviewing, including how to set up an effective staff selection process;
❑ managing the performance of new and existing staff;
❑ mentoring NQTs in their induction year;
❑ mentoring failing staff, identified either by inspection or by the school's appraisal systems.

These issues are dealt with in Chapters 8 to 10. The chapters set out strategies and processes for staff selection and interviews along with constructive advice on how best to manage the performance of individuals, from the youngest, most inexperienced member of staff to the longest serving. The changing profile of entrants into teaching now means that it is no longer a simple 'age is related to experience' equation. Career changers, mature entrants and early retirement from other professions mean that the newest, most inexperienced teacher may conceivably be the oldest in the department. Managing the performance of such varied staff is tricky but can be achieved with good guidance.

Conflict arises in all work-related situations and there is much to be made of the argument that conflict can be constructive if handled well. This area certainly provides the greatest challenge to new and existing managers. Dealing with conflict, which normally arises from the desire to implement change, is the subject of Chapter 11. The final chapters consider some legal and financial aspects of running a department, set within the framework of the *School Teachers' Pay and Conditions of Employment* document. Knowledge of this, and other guidelines in force, is crucial to knowing what the boundaries are that you, as a manager, have to remain within. This book is not authoritative legal advice and should not, therefore, be taken as such. It does, however, alert teachers and managers to the range of legal responsibilities that they must work within. The mere fact that the legal precedent of *in loco parentis* was established in 1893 and is still the overriding tenet of the duty of care teachers must exercise over their charges is remarkable, but the fact that teachers would have it no other way is a testament to their professionalism. No one would argue that on occasion the notion of *in loco parentis* has been abused by some parents, who either fail to support or abdicate responsibility for their offspring. In the role of departmental manager you will have a dual responsibility, not only to exercise a duty of care over your pupils, but also to exercise a duty of care over your staff.

IN CONCLUSION

At the outset of this introduction I stated that management is about people, not results, resources or retribution. Perhaps I should expand on this. If you manage people well – if you provide good leadership and the vision that is inherent to being a good leader – then the day-to-day management of resources will be guided by what the people need and want. The all-important results will come from the people for whom you have provided as a manager and leader. Manage as you would wish to be managed yourself. Make the phrase *'my staff are my most important resource'* mean something. The phrase is all too often spoken at staff meetings, and at the start and end of the school year, and it has an empty ring for many.

WHAT IS MANAGEMENT?

'"Management" means, in the last analysis, the substitution of thought for brawn and muscle, of knowledge for folklore and superstition, and of co-operation for force . . .'
Peter F. Drucker

This introductory chapter will look at the concept of management and briefly outline the development of management theory in general and look at the influences that have led to the introduction of management theory into the school setting. It will then consider the concept of the four spheres of management, determining, planning, organizing and measuring, before looking at management styles and addressing management principles as applied to individuals. The chapter ends with an attitude survey

AN INTRODUCTION TO MANAGEMENT THEORY

Once upon a time a zookeeper built a cage for five monkeys. In the cage the keeper hung a banana on a string just out of reach and put some steps underneath the banana. As soon as the keeper left the cage the five monkeys looked at the banana and began to jump up to get it. They couldn't reach the banana, but didn't give up. Soon, one of the monkeys went to the steps, intending to climb towards the banana. As soon as he touched the steps, the keeper sprayed all of the monkeys with ice-cold water. After a while, another monkey tried to climb the steps. The keeper again sprayed all the monkeys with ice-cold water. This happened several more times.

After some time, when a monkey tried to climb the steps, the other monkeys all tried to prevent him. Once this happened, the keeper turned the hose off and stopped spraying the monkeys. The next day the keeper removed one monkey from the cage and replaced it with a new one. The new monkey saw the banana and wanted to climb the steps. To his horror, all of the other monkeys attacked him. After another attempt and attack, he knew that if he tried to climb the steps, he would be assaulted.

Next, the keeper removed another of the original five monkeys and replaced it with a new one. The newcomer went to the steps and was attacked. The previous newcomer took part in the punishment with enthusiasm. Again, the keeper replaced a third original monkey with a new one. The new one made it to the steps and was attacked as well. Two of the four monkeys that beat him had no idea why they were not permitted to climb the steps, or why they were participating in the beating of the newest monkey, but they still took part anyway.

After replacing the fourth and fifth original monkeys, all the monkeys that had been sprayed with ice-cold water had been replaced by the keeper. Nevertheless, no monkey ever again approached the steps. Why not? Because that's the way they've always done it and that's the way it's always been around here.

The moral of this story is that offering a banana, no matter how tempting, won't be enough if there is fear of the unknown. In many cases of school-based management, this story will be familiar. Performance pay may be the banana and the subtle replacement of middle managers by the head-teacher who only appoints people who will attack on command, even if they don't know why they are attacking, will be familiar to some of those reading this book. The art and science of good management is relatively simple to master. It is based on respect, for yourself, for others and for those over whom you have authority.

The word manager is variously defined as

❑   a person controlling or administering a business or part of a business;
❑   a person controlling the affairs, training etc of a person or team in sports;
❑   a person regarded in terms of skill in management.

The concept of manager seems rooted either in a sporting or business context. Education is neither sport nor business, yet managers are seen to be crucial elements in raising standards of teaching and learning. So, let us begin by stripping away the pretensions of the title and see what management is about and, more crucially, why it is important to us as teachers.

Today, a teacher is not just responsible for teaching children. We talk of classroom management and the need to manage our time. Teachers who aspire to true management roles in schools are often not well versed in the science of business management. We are, after all, subject specialists in the secondary sector and polymaths in the primary sector. The rise of management in education was highlighted by the introduction of Local Management for Schools (LMS) and the need to be accountable for a range of things from examination results to finance. The first question to ask is: do you

Table 1.1 *Teacher or manager?*

TEACHER	MANAGER
I teach children	I manage my pupils' learning
I control my class	I manage my class
I do what I can when I can	I plan and manage my time as best I can
I have colleagues, not managers	I understand the line management hierarchy in my school

consider yourself a teacher or a manager? Consider the responses in Table 1.1 from educators and their view of their role. Which do you subscribe to? Can you place yourself directly into the manager column or the teacher column? Or are you really a mixture of both?

Management is an overused term. More precisely, manager is overused. In the commercial world it seems that entry level is a manager level, or if not entry level then just after it. A well-known store offered me the services of a 'packing manager' – not her official title, but one referred to by the 'checkout manager'. If I had a complaint I could see one of the 'customer service managers'. The problem with overuse is that it disguises the function of the manager. Schools can sometimes adopt similar strategies and the current vogue is 'Co-ordinator', perhaps moving towards 'facilitator', though as yet we have not moved towards the title of 'manager' for all but the newest recruits. For some people titles are important and they believe that what they do will be regarded as more important if they have a title. Some see the title, not the person, and, in other cases, the title may obscure the role, sometimes the crucial role, that the person may have. Regardless of our views on managers and management there is no doubt that in the schools of today management theory has its place, albeit somewhat modified from the world of business.

WHAT IS THE DRIVING FORCE FOR MANAGEMENT IN SCHOOLS?

A brief historical overview

The concept of management has not been accepted in education without its detractors and objectors. Gray (1984) describes an observed 'non effect' of management training skills in schools:

In over 13 years' work in this area I have come to the conclusion that, in broad terms at least, nothing is actually achieved by teaching management skills; schools just go on as they always have.

This must be seen in the context of what was happening in schools in 1984. There was no national curriculum and the notion of formal, regular inspection was not common. School management was a result of historical precedence. There was little to no training for departmental managers and it was exclusively learning on the job. All that was to change in the late 1980s with the advent of firstly GCSE and then the National Curriculum. The days of entering teaching, being thrown a well-worn copy of the syllabus and told to 'get on with it' were over. The notion of 'what happened behind the classroom door was the business of the teacher and no one else' was fast coming to an end. With increasing change came a need to manage that change. Headteachers and middle managers needed a strategic plan to implement the changes that were revolutionizing education in the late 1980s.

Table 1.2 briefly looks at the impact of three major changes to the education system in the 1980s and 90s. There is no doubt that the restructuring of education has increased the need for well-trained managers and the proposals of the recent government Green Paper *'Teachers: Meeting the Challenge of Change'* (DfEE, 1998) will add another strand to the role of management in education.

There are many references to management issues in the DfEE's Green Paper *Teachers: Meeting the Challenge of Change* (DfEE, 1998). Paragraph 34 sets out the government's intentions in modernizing the teaching profession. In relation to management they state that they intend 1) to recognize the role of teachers in raising standards, and 2) to create a culture in which all staff benefit from good quality training and development throughout their careers so that they can adopt proven best practice, develop innovative ideas and manage constant change.

Clearly an important focus here is about the management of change. Section 2 of the Green Paper addresses the issues of leadership and is concerned principally with the issue of whole school leadership, in particular that of the role of the headteacher. From now on, heads will have the responsibility for implementing the new performance management and pay system. Heads will not, however, be able to accomplish this in isolation from the other management levels within the school system. Here the departmental or subject leaders will have a role to play in appraisal, monitoring, review and the gathering of evidence for those teachers in their department or subject area who wish to break through the performance thresholds for main scale teachers and those set for the new Advanced Skills

Table 1.2 *The forces for change in schools*

LOCAL MANAGEMENT OF SCHOOLS (LMS)	THE NATIONAL CURRICULUM	INSPECTION
The changing role of the governing body	Managing introduction of NC and subsequent revisions (current revision 2000)	Assuming accountability for the curriculum and its effects on pupils' learning
Managing budgets	Fitting the NC to the school curriculum	Defining effectiveness
Staffing (full responsibility)	Deploying staffing	Responsibility for the standards of teaching and learning
Curriculum management	Cross-curricular themes	Individual teachers' accountability
School administration	Reporting NC outcomes	Assuming responsibility for 'value added'
Marketing of the school	Managing NC information (eg end of key stage tests)	Increasing public access to information
Managing parental choice and admissions procedures	Managing associated resources	Strategic deployment of resources
Autonomy in management of all budgets	Use of NC data to monitor effectiveness of teaching and learning	Responsibility for the impact of teaching and learning on pupil outcomes (eg public examination results and NC tests)
Estate management (ie maintenance, fixtures and fittings)	Managing the increased emphasis on NC outcomes	School effectiveness and 'value for money'
Income generation	League table positions	Positive inspection evidence/report

Teachers (ASTs). Allied to this will be the creation of a new leadership group in the management structure of the school. The leadership group may include ASTs and heads of major departments. The governing body will decide on the number of leadership group posts that a school will have and it will subsume the levels of management currently, including senior teachers and deputy heads. The governors will also determine the pay scale on which members of the leadership groups are promoted.

It is clear that the management structures of schools will be reformed and the role of the head of department will play a crucial part in the schools of tomorrow. The need for training and development of the role of the head of department is clearly stated in the Green Paper:

> The evidence points strongly to the importance of heads of departments and curriculum leaders in driving improvements in teaching and learning. We believe that schools should recognise their importance in allocating training budgets. Introductory leadership and manage- ment courses from the headship training programme should be avail- able to teachers who are taking on management responsibilities for the first time, whether or not they intend ultimately to aim for headship.

> (DfEE, 1998, para 53)

The new appraisal proposals will involve an annual assessment of perform- ance against agreed targets for all teachers. Clearly for managers and curriculum leaders this will involve assessment of their performance in management as well as actual teaching. If subject leaders and department heads are to be assessed on their performance as managers and comments made about the management of their areas, we must seek to define what management is and how management theory has developed over the past 150 years or so.

WHAT IS MANAGEMENT?

Definitions of management vary and, in truth, there is no one definition. One constant factor, however, has been the description of management in a business context. This is not surprising as the development of management theory over the past 150 years has been rooted in this context. Management as a concept in education is relatively recent. It is worth looking back at the development of management theory and the main theorists.

The classical theories of management, such as those proposed by Henri Fayol (1841–1925), in his seminal work *General and Industrial Management* (1949)[1], and F W Taylor (1856–1915) in *The Principles of Industrial Management* (1911), considered the organization of people in the workplace and the organization of the work itself. Fayol, a French industrialist, outlined six essential activities of management:

❑ Technical
❑ Commercial
❑ Financial
❑ Security
❑ Accounting
❑ Managerial

Fayol's first five activities were self-explanatory and were mostly concerned with specifics, such as buying, selling, raising capital, providing financial information and actual factory production of the goods. The sixth activity was relatively new to businesses. Managerial activities, contended Fayol, included elements of planning and organization and encompassed the notion of strategic deployment of personnel with a view to achieving an agreed plan of action. Fayol's definition of management then included the notion that people had a part to play in the management of a business, both from a top-down perspective and from the notion of having to strategically deploy people in the workforce to achieve the stated goals of the 'bosses'.

F W Taylor, on the other hand, developed a scientific approach to management. His background as an engineer and his experiences on the factory floor were the grounding he needed to develop his theory of 'scientific management'. The key to Taylor's definition of management lay in his quest for efficiency. Rather than run a factory on historical precedents, he looked for ways to develop a new, radical approach that would require workers and managers alike to embrace a different mindset and to think and operate more scientifically. From his experiences as a shop-floor worker he recognized that labourers were not working towards greater output and efficiency, as there was an element of self-preservation necessary that arose from fear. Essentially he identified the notion of 'soldiering' and classified it as either natural or systematic. Natural soldiering resulted from the tendency of workers to take things at a not so hectic pace, a tendency to be lazy. Systematic soldiering was a more deliberate act, the act of restricting the work rate. These fears, concluded Taylor, rested on three main reasons;

---

[1] *An English translation of his original 1916 work,* Administration industrielle et general.

unemployment, fluctuating income and restrictive methods of work allowed by management. Taylor identified five steps in his scientific management approach:

1. Replace restrictive methods with a scientific approach to work operations.
2. Scientifically determine the correct method and time required for each operation.
3. Remove responsibility from the workforce and introduce a management structure to accept that responsibility.
4. Train the workforce in the new methods of operation and/or select a new workforce.
5. Determine the new scientific method or approach.

Both Fayol and Taylor developed their theories of management from within a working situation, from the 'factory floor' as it were. Another early pioneer, Max Weber (1864–1920), developed the academic approach to management theory. Weber was interested in organizational structures and why workers followed the instructions of the managers. In other words, he was looking at the notion of authority and why people obeyed those who are in authority. He defined three basic types of authority: traditional, rational-legal and charismatic.

Weber defined traditional authority as the kind held by those in monarchy, ie the authority is granted by tradition or custom and holders have done no more than inherit their position, either directly through family or by right, and therefore their authority. He defined rational-legal authority as that conferred by the rules and regulations of the organization, with the person having been granted authority by right of his or her position and post. Charismatic authority came from the personal capabilities and character of the holder. This leads to loyalty from the co-workers and confidence in their abilities, regardless of the post that they hold.

Management has been variously described by many 'gurus' such as Peter Drucker, and usually in the context of business. Aspects of this can be applied to the education context, but schools are not a business. Even though many business practices, such as appraisal of workers (teachers) and constant monitoring of performance in relation to input and output measures are carried out, it is much better for the purposes of education to look at management in four spheres as shown in Figures 1.1 and 1.2.

In Sphere 1, Determining, the manager will have to determine the direction, aims and objectives of the department. This cannot be done in isolation from the school's overall aims, objectives and the direction as determined by the governors and the headteacher.

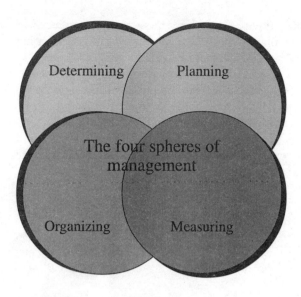

The four spheres of management

Determining Planning

Organizing Measuring

◈ **Figure 1.1** *The four spheres of management*

In Sphere 2, Planning, an important aspect will be planning for the achievement of the goals, aims and objectives set in Sphere 1. Simply talking or writing about what you as a manager would like to happen will not and cannot make this happen. The planning phase may be seen as the most crucial phase of management as future success may stand or fall by good planning. In some events this is no different from the basic tenet of good teaching – Good Planning. All experienced teachers will say that a well-planned lesson is more likely to succeed than an ill-planned lesson. It is important here to think about the success criteria that will be employed during the final measurement sphere. With no idea on how the success of a particular strategy may be indicated, the review and evaluation of the strategy employed is very difficult and may be open to misinterpretation.

Sphere 3, Organizing, takes in some of the practical issues of management such as available resources (staffing, time, materials etc), and the time frame required to complete the management of the proposed change/review.

Sphere 4, Measuring, allows the manager to determine the degree of success or otherwise of the implementation of the proposed change or a measurement of the effect of current practice on teaching and learning. This sphere will use the success criteria developed during the planning of the change or review strategy.

As Figure 1.1 implies, there is considerable overlap between the four spheres and elements of those spheres. To try to simplify management in a school situation would be to deny the complex nature of schools and the diversity of management structures that successfully coexist today. The imposition of one management structure and/or style on a school is undesirable. The collegiate nature of schools and education as a whole serves only to remind us that management cannot come from a centrally imposed model but must grow with the development and experience of its staff and community.

Within each of the spheres of management are distinct elements that direct the work of the manager (see Figure 1.2). The work of the manager is largely described within these four spheres, but it does not completely encompass all aspects of good management.

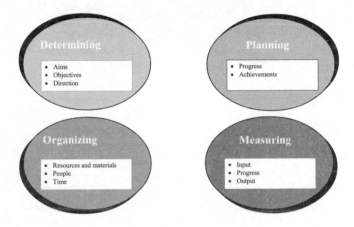

Figure 1.2 *Elements within the four spheres of management*

As a manager you will develop a style. Your style will be determined by a number of factors, not least your own experiences of being managed. It can be somewhat akin to being a parent. Many first-time parents will proclaim that they will never make the same mistakes as their own parents. Inevitably, many of their parents' traits and styles will be copied. So too will management styles that you experience be copied and tried until you develop your own style. There are many management style models. Two in particular have been employed for many years as basic models: Tannenbaum and Schmidt (1958) and Blake and Mouton (1964). Figures 1.3 and 1.4 illustrate these style models.

Tannenbaum and Schmidt's management style model considers a continuum between concern over results and concern about relationships. Along this continuum it is possible to identify four distinct management styles:

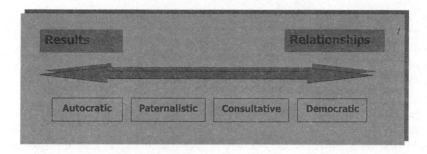

Figure 1.3 *The Tannenbaum and Schmidt management style model (1958)*

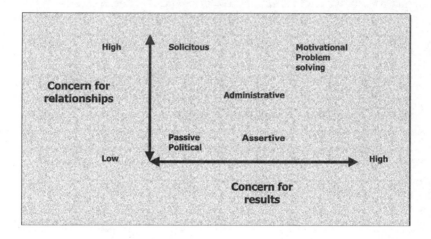

Figure 1.4 *The Blake and Mouton management style model (1964)*

1. Autocratic
2. Paternalistic
3. Consultative
4. Democratic

Each of these styles has positive and negative attributes and many good managers would argue that they display and utilize all of these styles according to the situation and management problem they are dealing with.

Blake and Mouton's model is more dimensional than Tannenbaum and Schmidt's, though there is still the relative concern for results and relationships. In this model there is scope for managers to decide on the level of concern for results and relationships. This model generates five management styles, categorized as:

1. Passive political
2. Solicitous
3. Administrative
4. Assertive
5. Motivational, problem solving

Again managers rarely display a single style but will adapt and utilize different styles according to the task that requires attention. It is true to say that people tend to favour one style over another and that their default style may be predominantly one of those illustrated.

Management and the use of one style over another are a delicate balancing act for many. The two main concerns for every manager in a school context are achieving results and developing relationships. Blake and Mouton's model more accurately reflects what actually happens in the workplace, as people will naturally be more or less concerned about results and relationships. In your own workplace you will be able to recognize the management styles exhibited not just by your own senior management teams but also by your colleagues in whatever role they are fulfilling, from learning support assistant to headteacher.

Figure 1.5 details the management style characteristics attributed to Blake and Mouton's model. It will be obvious that sticking to one style, regardless of circumstance, will lead to ineffectual management. The most successful managers utilize many of the characteristics listed in Figure 1.5 in order to achieve their desired goal.

Many and various social pressures can have a bearing on effective school management. Employment, stress, housing, cultural issues, deprivation, and many other factors can have an effect on how schools are, and should be, managed. Add to this the pressures directly facing schools, such as competition for pupils, league table positions and the management of the fabric of the school buildings, and it is easy to see that there are yet further pressures. The result is that schools need to respond to these and other pressures and issues with a coherent management strategy. West-Burnham (1997) states that there is a need to develop a coherent and systematic view of what the management of learning in schools means. He lists a number of symptomatic problems associated with management in schools:

❏ No clear or agreed criteria as to the components of school management.
❏ Unclear definitions of the purpose of senior and middle management.
❏ Deference to experience over skills and qualities.
❏ Limited access to management – the word is used as a collective noun rather than to describe a process.
❏ Training is often random, ad hoc and peripheral.

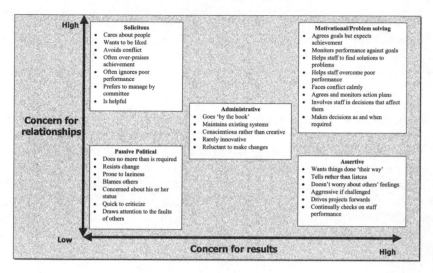

Figure 1.5 *Management style characteristics*

❏ Administrative procedures are seen as a substitute for effective management.

❏ Management as a process lacks a focus on learning.

What West-Burnham omits from this is the attitude of the manager towards the goals that the headteacher has identified as important for achieving his or her ultimate vision for the direction of the school. The following attitude survey, adapted from Everard and Morris (1996), investigates your feelings about the role and position you have at present. While this is in no way a definitive assessment of your current job satisfaction levels, it may be indicative of how you are feeling at present and may allow you to pinpoint areas where satisfaction levels are less than satisfactory. Try completing the survey and comparing your results to the tables in Appendix A, which give the results for a group of teachers based in normal state comprehensive schools in the London Metropolitan area. The staff was middle or aspiring middle managers undertaking training in middle management skills. Appendix A also provides an interpretation of the scores.

ATTITUDE SURVEY

Read each statement and circle the number that best describes your feeling about the statement. Add up your scores using the guide at the end of the survey.

Statement						
1. How often have you felt unable to utilize your full capabilities in your job?	Nearly always 0	Very often 1	Fairly often 2	Not often 3	Seldom 4	Never 5
2. How many functions do you perform in your job that you consider unimportant or unnecessary?	Nearly all 0	Most 1	Quite a few 2	A few 3	Very few 4	None 5
3. From your point of view, how often are you able to make worthwhile contributions?	Almost never 0	Seldom 1	Sometimes 2	Quite often 3	Many times 4	Unlimited 5
4. How often do you feel that your job is one that could be done away with?	Almost all of the time 0	Most of the time 1	Quite often 2	Very seldom 3	Almost never 4	Never 5
5. How much say do you think you have in determining how you do your job?	None 0	Almost none 1	Very little 2	Fairly large amount 3	Very large amount 4	Unlimited 5
6. How often have you felt that you could achieve more with more freedom to do the job your way?	Almost all the time 0	Most of the time 1	Quite often 2	Not very often 3	Very seldom 4	Almost never 5
7. How often have you received recognition for what you have done in your job?	Almost never 0	Very seldom 1	Not very often 2	Quite often 3	Very often 4	Many times 5
8. How often does your job give you the opportunity for personal recognition?	Almost never 0	Very seldom 1	Not very often 2	Quite often 3	Very often 4	Many times 5

	0	1	2	3	4	5
9. How do you feel about your job as a job where there is more to learn?	No more to learn	Nearly nothing to learn	Could learn something more	Can learn a little	Can learn a lot	Can learn a vast amount
10. What do you feel the school has to offer you in learning opportunities?	No chance to learn	Almost no chances	Can learn something	Can learn a little	Can learn a lot	Can learn a vast amount
11. How often have you inwardly felt that you have achieved something?	Very seldom	Once in a while	Fairly often	Often	Very often	All the time
12. To what extent is it possible to know how well you are doing in your job?	No way to know	Almost no way	To some extent	To a large extent	To a great extent	Entirely possible
13. To what extent is it possible to introduce new ideas in your work?	No extent	Almost no extent	Little extent	Fairly large extent	Large extent	Great extent
14. How often do you find your work interesting?	Never	Very seldom	Not very often	Quite often	Very often	Almost always
15. How often have you thought of either resigning or changing jobs?	Very often	Often	Fairly often	Once in a while	Very seldom	Never
16. To what extent do you consider your present post helpful for a person looking for promotion?	Definitely no help	Very little help	Some help	Fairly helpful	Very helpful	Extremely helpful

Survey scoring

Mark your score for each item in the groups shown below.

Question number	Group total	Group total average	Group name
1+3+11+13			Achievement
5+6			Responsibility
7+8+12			Recognition
16			Advancement
2+4+14+15			Work interest

Now compare your scores to the interpretation sheet in Appendix A.

IN CONCLUSION

Much has been written on management and management theory. The important elements to good and effective management are a clear idea of the aims and objectives that the manager has to achieve and the development of a coherent plan designed to achieve those goals. The measurement of success or degrees of success in achieving these goals is also crucial to effective management. It is analogous to a journey. Setting off without a destination and clear idea of the route will result in many wrong turns, much lost time and, ultimately, how will you know when you have arrived if you don't really know where you are going? You will most probably end your journey at a destination that may be comfortable but will always remain unfulfilling as you sit and wonder just where you might have ended up if you had travelled just that little bit further.

2

LEADERSHIP AND DECISION MAKING

'The very essence of leadership is that you have to have a vision.'
Theodore Hesburgh

This chapter will define leadership in the context of subject leadership and beyond and compare and contrast managers and leaders. It will then investigate the role of Power, Influence and Authority (PIA) and the PIA triangle in leadership. Finally it will explain the decision-making process and decision-making styles.

WHAT IS LEADERSHIP?

Leadership is now a central role of any management structure in a school. The new leadership group, announced in the Green Paper on education (DfEE 1998), reinforced the concept of leadership in schools. The central question is how leadership and management are related to each other and whether a good manager is a good leader and vice versa. There are a number of schools of thought in this area. Dynamic leadership is not always a sign of good management and not all good managers are dynamic. It is helpful to think about the roles of the manager as discussed in the last chapter and to consider the management styles outlined in Figures 1.3 and 1.4. In both of the management styles, results and relationships are the two axes along which the styles are placed. At no point do they consider aspects of leadership. A definition of leadership in a school context, but by no means the only one, is the ability, either directly or indirectly, to lead people by setting an inspiring example with the express aim of realizing the vision and values of the headteacher. The vision, and its associated values, as set out by the headteacher, should have been clearly communicated to the staff of the school. The leadership team of deputy heads and senior teachers has the task of further communicating that vision and how it is to be achieved to the subject leaders and middle management of the school. Your role as a middle manager is to put procedures into practice that work towards achieving the vision. Like the children's playground game of whispers, the more stages a message passes through, the more likely it is to become distorted. Similarly the vision, if not clearly communicated and reinforced regularly, may become distorted and blurred as it passes through the layers of management into the classroom. So can we define what leadership is and distil from this a set of skills and attributes for good leaders?

Good leadership is:

❏ inspirational;
❏ persuasive;
❏ beneficial for the common good;
❏ indirect.

Leadership is not about:

❏ motivation;
❏ coaching;
❏ development of others' skills;
❏ planning;
❏ organizing.

Bennett (1995) states that 'leadership gives direction to the work of others, helping them to see what is wanted in a particular setting, and how it should be achieved'. He goes on to say that there is a separation of 'leadership' from 'work'.

THE GRAIN PIT

Interestingly, we find natural leaders in all walks of life and some people, even from a very young age, may have leadership qualities that become apparent. The Science Museum in London had an interactive display called 'The Grain Pit' as part of their interactive science gallery 'Launch Pad'. During its development, various exhibits were put out on trial to see how the target audience, Key Stage 2 children, would receive them. The display required children to co-operate in transporting grain around a series of pits using different mechanical means to move the grain. There was an Archimedes screw, a conveyor belt, a small shovel and various handles to turn that scooped up grain and deposited it elsewhere. It required a team effort to move the grain and, invariably, the children working in the pit were not known to each other and were brought together by accident, having been invited in at random to try out the ideas. It required four people to get the pit working efficiently. Some days the pit was a hive of activity and the children worked hard for what was little reward. The construction of the pit meant that grain merely moved around from place to place, ending up where it started, in a holding area. There was no reward other than to see a continuous flow of grain moving around the structure. When a team took up the challenge they invariably did work hard. When the team was broken, when a child left either through boredom or because another exhibit attracted attention, the result could be devastating as the flow was interrupted until a replacement could be found. When the pit was working at its best there was invariably a leader, and the leader had a vision of an uninterrupted, even flow of grain moving smoothly around. Sometimes the leader was not even in charge of an action or a device; he or she simply communicated the vision. The leader explained to the team that the way the exhibit was supposed to work was by achieving this uninterrupted flow – it wasn't actually the intention of the designers, they were more interested in the scientific principles it displayed – so he or she would walk around the pit pointing this out, inspiring the others to work as hard as they could to achieve the goal. On other days, the exhibit was not fulfilling. Then there was no coherence and direction to the work and children merely were fascinated by how a particular device or part of the pit worked, giving no consideration to any other part of the exhibit. The children who climbed aboard this exhibit and played were no more than upper Key Stage 2 age, yet they could be readily grouped into three categories

Leaders with vision

These are the children who directed the work of others, usually appointing managers to sections of the exhibit. They spent their time calling for the speeding up or slowing down of various components. Their vision was one of seeing the grain flow around the exhibit at a constant rate, uninterrupted if at all possible. A constant flow of grain was their goal.

The natural managers

During the times that natural managers were in sole charge of the pit (usually occupying the highest level from where they could direct the others), children worked hard but the even consistent flow was never achieved. The manager didn't communicate his or her vision to the others – assuming, that is, that the manager did indeed have a vision at all. The pit invariably shuddered to a halt and interest in the exhibit was lost. The natural managers needed the leader with vision in order to achieve the full potential of the exhibit.

The workers

These children only concentrated on their device and were more concerned with productivity and shifting as much grain as possible.

After many hours of observing children playing on the grain pit it became clear that there were indeed leaders, managers and workers. If a leader decided that he or she needed to move on to another exhibit, having completed his or her task, others in the team could assume the role of leader having watched and learnt from the original leader. If this did happen, it often meant that a new team had to be built up, as, with the departure of the leader, some of the team also left. In its simplified way this is a model for leadership and management in schools. In those schools with an inspirational leader, with a clear and well-communicated vision, the team can work well in moving towards realizing that vision. When an inspirational headteacher leaves, there is often a large turnover of staff. In a school with a core of good managers but no real leadership and vision, the team often work very hard towards a series of separate goals with some success along the way but with many false starts and little coherence. The ideal, then, would be a school with inspirational leadership communicating a clear vision and values, with layers of management who motivate, direct, plan and organize the work of others into realizing the vision and its associated values.

The distinction between leaders and managers can often be blurred but may be summed up as follows: leadership is about the direction of people for the solution of problems, whereas management is about the manoeuvring of money and materials to the solution of problems. It is important to note here that leaders may not be concerned about the people who will solve the problem but good managers, as well as manoeuvring money etc, will be concerned about the people they manage.

LEVELS AND TYPES OF LEADERSHIP

Leadership is not a single operation, carried out in one particular way or in one particular style. In essence there are three levels of leadership:

❏ strategic;
❏ operational;
❏ individual.

All three levels of leadership will come into play at one time or another in the management of a department. Strategic leadership relates to the overall vision and direction of a department and strategic leadership allows for the setting of clear goals. Operational leadership is required for the interpretation of school policies into workable procedures. Good heads of department/subject leaders can use this layer to emphasize how they lead by example, by consistently following the procedures and practices laid down and agreed. Individual leadership works by heads of department or subject leaders inspiring team members and sustaining morale.

Cole (1996) characterizes leaders into five types and links leadership with behaviour. The five types are described in behavioural terms and he regards leadership as a dynamic, not static, process. This provides a useful contrast to the process of management that is, in practice, often static and not dynamic. The notion of the manager sitting at their desk, planning, organizing the work of others, preparing rotas of staffing, topics, timetables etc is a familiar one and provides a distinction between management and leadership.

Cole's leadership types can be summarized as:

1. *Traditional leader.* The position of this type of leader is often one assumed by birth right, as in the case of the monarchy, tribal leaders or, on a more down to earth note, succession in a business passing from the parent to their offspring.
2. *Situational leader.* The skill displayed by this type of leader relies on being in the right place at the right time. Their leadership success is often not transferable to other situations and, as a result, their influence on an organization is often limited.
3. *Appointed leader.* Many managers are in this group, where their leadership influence arises from their appointment to a position. The appointment of a subject leader in a school in a sense automatically makes the appointed person the leader of the group. In fact the national standards refer to subject leadership rather than subject management. In many cases the appointment and its associated job specification and

description (see Chapter 10) heavily concentrates on management issues rather than the more difficult role of leadership.

4. *Functional leader.* These leaders secure their influence by their actions. It is entirely possible for a functional leader to operate without the security of an appointed position.
5. *Charismatic leader.* The key factor in the success of this type of leader is their personality. In effect this group contains the 'natural leaders'. These are the people who can exert influence over many people, sometimes from many spheres of life, and who attract natural followers. Many historical figures, both heroes and villains, are examples of natural leaders: Winston Churchill, Adolf Hitler, and more recent examples, the likes of Richard Branson and Bill Gates.

It would be wrong to think that a leader and leadership are limited to one style. Elements of at least three of the types may be learned and put into operation, but the fifth, the charismatic leader, has qualities and traits that cannot be learnt, only modified (Cole, 1996).

LEADERSHIP STYLES

The simplest way of looking at leadership style is to consider the variables that affect how leaders work. They are:

1. the leader;
2. the task;
3. the team;
4. the environment.

The interactions of these four key variables will define the situation that the leader has to cope with. Their style, both in leadership and management terms, will be defined by these variables and the approach that they take as a leader will also depend on them. When we considered management styles in Chapter 1, we looked at two models, the Tannenbaum–Schmidt management continuum and the Blake–Mouton style positions. Similarly, in looking at leadership styles we can consider two further models, the Tannenbaum–Schmidt continuum of leadership (Figure 2.1) and Reddin's 3D approach (Figure 2.2).

The Tannenbaum–Schmidt model is limited in that it is really concerned with the degree of freedom team members have related to the authoritarian/democratic behaviour of the leader or manager.

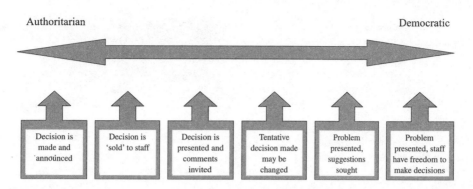

Figure 2.1 *Leadership styles and decision making*

As you move from the authoritarian end to the democratic, you will see that the level of freedom enjoyed by the team increases to the point where complete freedom to make decisions is enjoyed. Again we are left with the impression that these are styles that are fixed. In truth there may be a range of leadership styles presented by managers, depending on the task or decision to be made. It is often the case, however, that a leader will predominantly display and operate one or two styles.

Reddin's 3-D theory builds on Blake and Mouton's management grid (Figure 1.5), extending their grid into a 3-D model. His two main axes are Task Orientated and Relationship Orientated, with the third dimension being added as a measure of effectiveness, from more effective to less effective.

The interesting aspect Reddin includes in his grid is that of taking account of the appropriateness of the situation. By considering four basic styles, Related, Separated, Integrated and Dedicated, he then derives a further eight styles, four accompanying inappropriate situations, Missionary, Deserter, Compromiser and Autocrat, and four to accompany appropriate situations, Developer, Bureaucrat, Executive and Benevolent Autocrat. It is self-evident that appropriate situations within which the leader can function will lead to styles that are more effective. Situations where good managers and leaders are taken out of situations where they are comfortable and knowledgeable can invoke any of the four inappropriate styles. A situation common in industry is the head hunting of chief executives into industry situations where they have little to no knowledge. The danger here is that inappropriate situations can lead the head-hunted executive to under-perform or to perform in a leadership style that results in failure. The new chief executive becomes a missionary determined to promote the worth of the company beyond its actual position, or they will desert after a

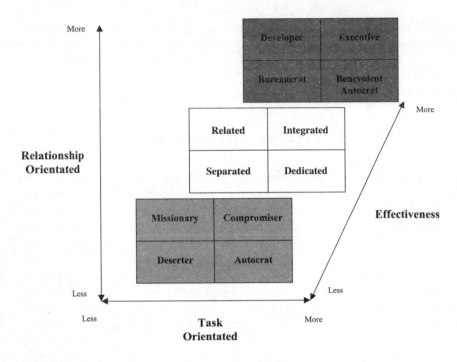

Figure 2.2 *Reddin's 3-D model, adapted from Cole (1996)*

short period of time, leaving unfinished restructured management and redefined goals that have not been clearly communicated to the employees. A real danger here lies in schools that have been subjected to a new start or fresh start. So-called super-heads will be appointed to turn the school around. While these headteachers have shown a high degree of success in their own self-built schools, taking them to a new, perhaps inappropriate situation can lead to the development of inappropriate leadership. Early in 2000 a succession of 'super-heads' left their schools, leading to the supposition that they had in fact been placed in inappropriate situations. The effect may then be for them to display any or all four of the inappropriate leadership styles.

A danger to new and aspiring heads of department is the notion that any middle management job will be appropriate for them. It is vital that middle managers are aware of their own abilities and to consider applications for heads of department jobs with great care, so as to avoid falling into the inappropriate situation category.

Another model of leadership was developed by John Adair, Functional Leadership, based on the notion that leadership is linked more to behaviour than to other, less tangible attributes such as 'a natural born leader'. Adair's model sees the whole task to be undertaken in terms of the needs of the task, the group and individuals, and that any leadership must weigh the concerns of all three before the whole situation can be appraised and a procedure found to achieve the task.

MAKING DECISIONS

On the surface, the ability to make decisions seems relatively simple. A simplistic scientific approach may be adopted that means the manager or leader defines a problem, gathers information, assesses the merits of various solutions and makes a decision. In theory this simplistic approach should work. It is, after all, something that all of us do on a day-to-day basis. The problem is that we are attending a party and do not know what to wear, casual, smart, formal etc. We gather information, where the party is, when it is to take place, other guests who may be at the party, and we decide on what is appropriate dress. The problem is that occasionally we receive either mixed messages or incorrect information and this could result in the wrong decision. A classic example is the hilarious sketch from the BBC series *Only Fools and Horses* where Del Boy and Rodney are invited to a party, which they are initially told is fancy dress. They turn up as Batman and Robin only to find that there has been a death and the party is now a funeral gathering. It makes for one of the funniest clips on television, but illustrates just how easily even a simple decision can go wrong.

In teaching, our decisions will rarely if ever be as hilarious or inappropriate but given the complex nature of teaching, many seemingly simple decisions can have knock-on effects that may have major repercussions. Providing inaccurate information to the school timetabler may cause insurmountable problems in the allocation of staff to groups. Similarly, if the timetabler does not use the correct information it could result in a less than effective timetable. Being a head of department or middle manager in a school means that you will frequently have to make decisions on many matters. If you have been appointed to the role, then you have, by default, been given the authority to make these decisions. The staff in your team will expect you to make the decisions. They will often take it for granted when you make the right (to them) decision as this is seen to be one of your responsibilities. If, however, you make a wrong decision, then they will be quick to let you know, either face to face or less subtly, by their actions. The problem with decision making is summed up in the old adage, 'You can fool some of the people all of the time and all of the people some of the time, but you can't fool all of the people all of the time' (Abraham Lincoln).

Making decisions means that you have a degree of authority. In the case of appointed leaders and managers, that authority is granted with the post. Being a good manager is not about accepting the authority and using it without careful thought, but showing your team that the authority granted to you is properly exercised. There are three aspects to decision making: power, influence and authority.

Power is defined as the ability to influence, influence is a process and authority is the right to use power. By looking carefully at how these three aspects interrelate, we can vary our decision-making styles to suit the situation and the team for which we have responsibility. Figure 2.3 shows power, influence and authority and relates this to the decision-making styles associated with relative degrees of each aspect. In theory, a manager should use a consultative style wherever team commitment is required. The problem is that if all decisions were consultative then nothing would ever be effected as most of the team's time would be taken up in consultative exercises. Team commitment is critical to success but can be achieved even when autocratic decision-making styles are employed. This relies on the manager knowing what style to use on what type of decision. Trivial decisions do not need consultation (e.g. the colour of exercise books, the type of pens and pencils available to staff in the team). When dealing with professionals, team commitment is harder to obtain than in non-professional situations. In the case of teachers, their knowledge of the issues surrounding decisions is often high and they are in their own right more than capable of reaching and making decisions after weighing up the information on offer. Important decisions are therefore mainly made on a partnership basis; multiple input into the decision-making process by expert members of the team is essential. If we take the case of a core specialist subject such as science, most heads of science are not expert in all sciences to A level. As a result they will have to rely on the expert input of a subject specialist to advise on, say, a decision to change from one syllabus to another. The same is true for the head of humanities whose expertise in all humanities subjects is limited. The notion of top-down decision-making processes – autocratic – is mainly reserved for labour-intensive industries. In schools the notion of the leader as sole decision maker should by now be virtually obsolete. Even in the case of headteachers who appear to make only autocratic decisions, it is invariably the result of multiple input from senior and middle management layers.

Decision making can be approached in a scientific way, but this by no means guarantees that the right decision will be made each and every time. Figure 2.4 describes a decision-making process that can be used by middle managers. The ten steps allow for a participative approach if necessary, but step 3 allows the manager to decide on the extent of expert input

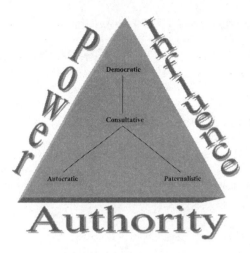

Figure 2.3 *The Power, Influence, Authority triangle*

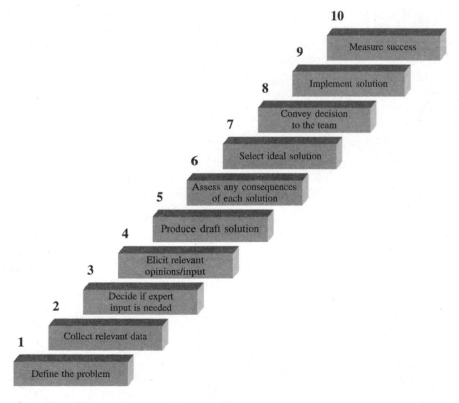

Figure 2.4 *The ten-step decision-making process*

needed. At this stage, the manager could decide that no expertise other than their own is needed and so proceed to a decision without consultation. This would be entirely appropriate for some situations, but not for others where important decisions that may affect the rest of the team need to be taken.

One of the most common sources of failure to succeed when implementing strategies is a failure to involve team members in decisions that may affect their working practices or conditions. When deciding if expert input is needed at stage 3, be aware of the impact that the decision may have on the working conditions of those charged with either implementing a new strategy or having to deal with the new work practices.

3

TIME MANAGEMENT

'Time is an illusion. Lunchtime doubly so.'
Douglas Adams

In this chapter we will consider how time management can help us create a purposeful working environment and limit the effects of wasting working time. It will consider ways in which time is used inefficiently and look at ways in which time can be used more efficiently to satisfy the demands of teaching and management.

There are two positions to consider when dealing with time management. Either you are constantly saying 'but I don't have enough time to…' or you have no problem. There are many issues to deal with when considering time management and much has been written on the subject, from complex academic texts to a 'Dummies' Guide'. There is no text, however, on the subject of time management in schools that I am aware of. This creates a problem from the start because, as a teacher and education-based manager, you will find much of the advice given in time management books hard to follow. Take as an example the following extract from *The Complete Idiot's Guide to Managing Your Time* (Davidson, 1999):

> To sustain the habit of leaving work on time, start with a small step. For example decide that on every Tuesday you will stop working on time and take no extra work home with you. After freeing up Tuesdays for a whole month, perhaps add Thursdays. In another month add Mondays, in the fourth month add Wednesdays. (p 7)

Many teachers would simply laugh at the idea of sustaining this regimented approach to making sure that work only takes place during 'working hours'. The nominal school day is 5 hours of contact time for pupils, resulting in 25 hours per week on average. In secondary education we are not required normally to teach for 25 hours per week, but the non-contact time available to you will vary from school to school. In the primary sector the position is different, with little to no non-contact time. Even if we were to extend this 25-hour working week to a nominal 40-hour week, to reflect common work practices outside education, it would mean an average of 3 hours per day per teacher, outside normal school hours, spent on meetings, administration etc. It is obviously impossible, even for the most efficient of teachers, to work to a 40-hour week and complete all of the teaching, non-teaching and administrative tasks that are required. If you add to this the responsibility of managing a team, the 40-hour week evaporates without trace. The problem is how much time is enough? When should you metaphorically down tools and spend time on your own life? Clearly you cannot devote all of your time to teaching and management and there must be a cut-off point. Many teachers feel that no matter how hard or how long they work they will be unable to complete all of their tasks. To begin with, we need to identify where the time goes in our crowded day/week. We also need to identify what is in effect time wasting and what are time-wasting activities.

The following exercise requires some of your valuable time. Although this task at first sight seems simply to impose another task on an already busy schedule, it can in the long run identify significant areas where time is being 'wasted' or where work practices are not efficient.

ACTIVITY LOG

In order to identify where time is being wasted it is necessary to log a typical working week. Your week will be divided between:

❑ teaching (denoted as contact time; this includes cover work);
❑ prescribed time (eg attendance at meetings, break/lunch duty);
❑ administrative time (filling in required paperwork, replying to memos from others, dealing with mail etc);
❑ planning for teaching (including lesson-planning time, research time for subjects etc);
❑ marking (marking of pupil work, homework, tests etc);
❑ discretionary time (seeing pupils to offer advice, overseeing detentions, running extra-curricular activities).

Draw up a log for a typical week at work. Try to avoid examination periods or points where there is a substantial but temporary change to the timetable (see Appendix B for a suggested template) and complete the log to identify the proportions of your time taken on the various tasks. For ease you can display the results as a bar chart or pie chart. This will help you to visualize where the time is being spent. The next analysis that needs to be done is to look at what takes up the most time. As you make your way up the management ladder in a school, the proportion of administrative time will inevitably increase. What is not inevitable is that the proportion of teaching time will decrease to the same extent. Looking at your results, can you see where time goes? There are some things that you cannot easily change, for example the amount of contact time and the marking. But what about those elements where you or your line manager may have some control, such as meetings, administrative work or prescribed tasks? Are these being carried out with the greatest efficiency? Is every meeting necessary and is every piece of paper you fill in absolutely essential?

If you look carefully at the log you can begin to work out some interesting statistics:

❑ What percentage of your week is directly involved in contact with children?
❑ What percentage of your time is spent on administration?
❑ What percentage of your time is spent on work at home?

Many interesting variations on these questions can arise. The log should really be a focus and should reflect your priorities. Taking things a stage further, it would be interesting to look at your job description and compare what you should be doing with what you actually are doing. Is the job description realistic? Does it need looking at and perhaps changing to reflect what you are actually doing? The log must not, however, be viewed as a driving force for change in your work practices. You must seek to identify your priorities and the priorities of the school. If anything, it may be a shift in your perception of the job you do that needs to take place, rather than a change in the job itself.

TIME WASTERS

Effective and efficient use of time really depends on the reduction of time-wasting activities and procedures. There are, of course, people that we often refer to as time wasters, and developing good communication skills (see Chapter 6) will help in ensuring that they are not part of the problem we have as managers.

Common time wasters are:

❑ incomplete or missing information;
❑ team members with problems;

❑ lack of delegation;
❑ the telephone;
❑ routine tasks;
❑ lunch;
❑ interruptions;
❑ meetings;
❑ lack of priorities;
❑ management by crisis;
❑ outside activities;
❑ poor communication;
❑ mistakes.

Although all could be classified as time wasters, some are important, such as sorting out the problems of team members. The question is, where and when is this appropriate, and are you the best person to seek advice from? Some teachers even see lunch as a time waster as so many things have to be done. But taking a break is important, even if it is just 15 minutes out of a busy day to sit and reflect. Remember, a working day with no break is illegal! The list above is just indicative and you will be able to add to this list and may even disagree with some of it. Try making your own list and then seeing what can be done about minimizing the impact of those things you regard as time wasting.

Time management is not always something we can control independently of others and independently of the organization within which we operate. Figure 3.1 shows the main elements that contribute to the management of time. Some of these are directly under your control, such as your ability to complete the tasks using skills acquired, but most are not.

The school culture/organization

If you remember the zookeeper story on page 1, then you will appreciate that many schools have policies and procedures as a matter of historical precedence. It is important that the management of the school check on the effectiveness of their procedures on a regular basis. What was, at one time, an effective procedure might now only exist because that's the way it has always been done. The effective middle manager carries out the same reviews periodically to ensure that neither they nor their staff are following unnecessary procedures. Is the system for referring pupils along the discipline line still relevant? Are the staff being required to complete paperwork that is no longer necessary? As a part of the government's pledge

Figure 3.1 *Factors affecting time management*

to teachers on its election to government, a review of the bureaucratic burdens on teachers was carried out and advice given to headteachers (DfEE, 1998). This advice listed ways in which the burdens on teachers could be reduced. Allied to this circular is a Web site devoted to publishing examples of good practice that aim to reduce the amount of duplication and paperwork that occurs in schools.

An analysis of working practices in the school is best undertaken by the middle management as it often falls to this level to produce the paperwork and deal on a day-to-day basis with many non-essential tasks. Simple time-saving procedures can be put in place with the agreement of middle managers and the overall school management, such as the maintenance of set lists of pupils centrally. It requires commitment from staff in providing up-to-date information and commitment from administrative staff to ensure that lists are provided efficiently and quickly or placed on the school network so that they can be accessed centrally. Having lists in various file formats eases the restrictions on the use of set lists as they can be down-loaded and transferred into various programs as the department wishes. If you calculate the amount of hours wasted by teachers typing duplicate information on pupils (and the potential for errors in the spelling of pupils' names) then it seems so obvious.

You

You are the key to effective time management, but are you equipped with the skills and knowledge you need in order to be effective? It may well be that your role as a manager is asking more of you than your role as a teacher. Are your keyboarding skills up to the task? Can you operate the spreadsheet package on your PC effectively to allow you to enter and produce the statistical information you require for the development plans, reports and end of year figures? Staff INSET is a difficult subject as there is rarely enough money and opportunity for staff to enhance their teaching skills, their understanding of learning, or their acquisition of the latest information on their subject without you demanding basic training in keyboard skills or software usage/basic statistics. Yet your needs as a manager are just as important as the needs of your staff. The natural tendency is to eliminate what you and what you suspect others see as 'non-essential' training. However, if you think rationally, acquiring the skills to effect your role more efficiently will have a knock-on effect in many quarters, even if your staff see it as you being better equipped to fight for their interests in senior management meetings. Before taking up a management post or shortly afterwards, you must audit your own needs and ensure that you have your fair share of INSET designed to meet your needs.

Other less tangible factors may rest on your own personal preferences such as the time of day when you work best (early morning, late night etc), the pace at which you work, for example concentrated effort in a sustainable period, or less concentrated over a longer period.

How much and when you delegate tasks can also lead to more effective time management. The natural tendency is to believe that as the manager you are responsible for everything and therefore must do everything in order to discharge that responsibility. This is not the case. By good effective delegation of tasks to others you will not only increase the efficiency of the department or team but you will also be providing opportunities for other staff to gain experience that will help their continuing professional development.

The job description

Many job descriptions are historical. Good schools will be reviewing job descriptions as a matter of course when staff are appraised. How up to date is the job description you hold? When was it last reviewed, and does it still reflect the job that you currently do? Often as new tasks are undertaken they are not added to the job description and when a review does eventually take place the actual job that you or a member of your team does may not bear much relation to the job description. Job descriptions, however, have a legal standing and cannot simply be changed or applied without proper recourse to consult with the individuals concerned. By reviewing the job description and updating it with all those little jobs and tasks that have been acquired, it is easy to see whether or not what is being asked of you or a team member is realistic given the time and resources available.

Your team

Your team can be a major time-consuming commodity in a less than efficient and happy working situation. An important issue is job prioritization. Your team will be looking to you to give the lead on prioritizing the demands of the senior management. By setting out their priorities you can avoid unnecessary time wasting as the team are all working to the same agenda. If the priority is teaching and learning, as it should be, then issues of coat wearing and trainers, which deflect from teaching and learning, should be dealt with outside the teaching and learning environment. It is no good individuals demanding the highest possible standards of dress and uniform adherence when the rest of the staff do not consider this a priority. The one teacher fighting the bulk of pupils will result in much wasted time. It is far better for staff and management alike to produce a coordinated plan to tackle issues and to ensure consistency across the school than the often called for, but rarely successful, 'crackdown'. Many teacher hours are wasted trying to enforce 'crackdowns' on a wide range of pupil misdemeanours such as gum, coats, trainers, make-up etc only for the crackdown to fail as the original impetus fizzles out after a short period of time. Deciding on a strategy and implementing this across the school is far more effective. Consider the following strategy for dealing with trainers.

An end to trainers?

One South London school decided to end the incidence of pupils wearing trainers to school, something that was expressly forbidden in the school rules. Instead of issuing the 'crackdown on trainers' for all staff to implement, resulting in much wasted time as staff fought with pupils to change out of trainers, a simple order went out to staff, parents and pupils alike. The school purchased very cheaply various sizes of black plimsolls – the sort found in the PE kits of many primary children from the 1960s – which were kept by the school office and were capable of being washed. The following notice went out to all staff and pupils.

> The school uniform code forbids the wearing of trainers in school except for specified activities. Any pupils wearing trainers will, on the authority of the Head, be sent to the school office where they will have their trainers and shoes (if pupils have them) substituted for school plimsolls to be worn for the rest of the day. Trainers and shoes will be returned at the end of the day. Repeated offences will result in detentions with school community service (picking up litter etc).

After the first few pupils were made to wear the very unfashionable plimsolls it had an amazing effect on the rest of the school and trainer wearing was virtually eradicated overnight.

This simple strategy was implemented with little fuss. It saved staff time as they were not required to oversee the changing of trainers and had the full backing of the head to enforce the notice. Pupils soon realized that it was much easier to obey the rule than to be singled out as a 'sad' plimsoll wearer. No staff time was taken with detentions for wearing trainers, as the punishment was to allow the pupils to fully participate in the school day, but with the 'sad' plimsolls and not the 'cool' trainers.

The pupils and parents

As the above account suggests, pupils can be a large influence on your time management. Dealing with the pupils, from teaching them to disciplining them, takes time. There are also restrictions on when certain things can be done. You will only have access to the pupils for certain periods of the day and despite your best efforts you will find it difficult to deal with them much beyond the school day. Many teachers will resort to dealing with pupils and parents out of school hours as this allows them freedom to contact parents at a time that is convenient to the member of staff. There are advantages and disadvantages to this. Contacting parents at inconvenient times may result in the parent taking issue with the pupils and reinforcing your demands of them. It can, however, backfire if the parent's evening is interrupted by a teacher with what the parent considers to be a trivial matter. It may then have the reverse effect. As a head of department you will necessarily have to deal with many parents on a range of issues. Sometimes you will be contacted about such matters as detentions set by your staff, test results, set movements etc. It mostly happens when there appears to be least time to deal with the problem. Although many parents will be forceful in demanding your time immediately and on their terms, a far better strategy is to arrange to call or meet the parent at a more convenient time, thus allowing you to gather information and background to the complaint before being pushed or bullied into making rushed, inappropriate decisions. The same is also true of pupils. Dealing with pupils on a 'when they appear' basis can lead to inefficient use of your time. A balancing act and a quick appraisal of the situation is required so that you can deal with problems efficiently. Supporting your team when they require your intervention on a discipline matter is vital to good management. This does not mean, however, that you must be at their beck and call and drop everything to sort out their problems as and when they arise. Putting in place a transparent, fair and effective discipline procedure that your team can use is a far better solution.

Your peers

Your peers can be your best friends and your worst enemies. A key task for the senior management of any school is to put in place an effective middle management. After all, the middle management layer is the one that can make or break a school. By creating a middle management layer that works as a team and is supportive of each other and supportive of the senior management, schools can make the greatest impact on teaching and learning. Too often there is an air of competition between departments that can impede progress to better and higher achievements. If the senior management is constantly goading heads of department about their results in the face of other departments' results, the endpoint is one of non-cooperation and frustration. Broadly speaking, the subjects should perform to approximately the same level, but this is by no means cut and dried. Even a simple comparison of end of key stage results in the core subjects reveals discrepancies. After all, maths is maths and science is science and there is no reason why pupils should achieve absolutely identical results in two different subject areas. This merely ignores the basic fact that some children like and perform better in some subjects than in others. Much time is wasted doing pupil-by-pupil comparisons and trying to find out why a pupil with a grade A in English didn't achieve the same in science. A much better approach would be to direct the energy of the middle management into looking at common ground and utilizing the best practice of each subject area across the school. Identifying common teaching approaches to common things such as graph drawing in maths and science and comprehension exercises in English and history is a far more useful and less time-wasting activity. Dealing with your peers requires excellent communication skills and knowledge of their needs and priorities. If their needs and priorities are clear and communicated to all, then your responses to them will be more useful and effective. Developing a coordinated approach to a range of issues is another way of ensuring more efficient time management.

Outside influences

The media constantly remind teachers of the outside influences that impact on our everyday practices. In the past 15 years there have been so many reforms, initiatives, changes and impositions that many teachers have left the profession, unable to deal with the stresses that successive governments have imposed. Day after day, many new brochures, notices, advisory letters, consultations and curriculum advice publications land on our desks. A major problem is directing where the material should go. Many teachers complain that much of the information does not reach them and others complain that too much reaches them. The school office often has an impossible task, trying to decide who should receive what and when. Many teachers fail to respond to consultative documents, as they simply do not have the time. Others reasonably rely on their professional associations to respond on their behalf. The fact is that no one has the time to read, digest and respond to all of the issues that arise from central, local and national government organizations. Yet as a manager you will need to keep abreast of what is happening. Early in 2000 the Qualifications and Curriculum Authority (QCA) published for the first time suggested schemes of work for many of the subjects at Key Stage 3. These are all available on the Internet in a downloadable form that schools could use and adapt to meet their own circumstances. Yet how many schools have produced schemes of work since it was announced that they would be available, and consumed many hours of development and word processing time when they could have waited and adapted instead? Many new textbooks have associated Web sites and access to materials that make the job of running a published scheme easier and faster and more adaptable than has previously been the case (Heslop, Brodie and Williams, 2000).

As a young teacher I once asked my first headteacher how he could possibly keep up to date on the latest initiatives and advice coming from the then Department for Education and Science (DES). His reply was simple and it is advice that to this day has served me well. He told me that he didn't actually read all of the documentation that came into his office. He immediately looked for an executive summary or turned to the conclusion section. Here, he said, you would find all of the important information, all of the key points. If it wasn't included here, then it probably wasn't important. Only at a later date when a specific issue or problem came to light did he ever delve into the main body of the text to look for specific answers.

Since the advent of the Internet there has never been so much information freely available to all. The charge that information never gets to the right person must be diminished now as much of the information is freely and quickly available on various Web sites hosted by the major government departments and interested bodies. Time spent keeping up to date with what is happening and what is planned may save time in the long run. It may also save money.

Replying to consultations is time consuming, but unless the main body of the teaching force has its say in shaping the future of the profession and of the curriculum, we will have no one else to blame but ourselves if the result is not what we hoped for. Change after the event is highly unlikely, and to effect change you must be heard from within. Regular communication of the latest events, policies and procedures is a role that as a middle manager you must take on. It is likely that some agenda items in your department meeting cycles will be given over to responses to government initiatives. By empowering the team to respond you will strengthen the team from within.

Your line manager

Your immediate line manager will have demands on you and on your time. By ensuring from the start that when meetings between you are called they are necessary, and not just the fulfilment of a neat paper-based cycle, you will save time. It is also important to set out the demands that each of you has of the other. Knowing who has the authority to deal with discipline or other matters can save time on both sides. If pupils are sent to your line manager by one of your staff, bypassing you, it could potentially waste your time and the time of your line manager. Clear procedures and clear responsibilities are vital to ensure that time is not wasted. Many issues that would otherwise be communicated by face-to-face meetings could be communicated with a simple memo system that copies information to the line manager. Beware, however, of copy overload where irrelevant material is passed on; this is also a waste of time and resources. Developing faith, trust and respect between line managers allows you the freedom to carry out the job to which you have been appointed and frees up time for you to do the job more effectively. If newly appointed to a middle management post, the earlier you set a meeting to discuss these matters the better. An annual review of procedures is also a useful way of making sure that you do not simply do something because 'that is what has always been done'.

IN CONCLUSION

The symptoms of poor time management are crisis management where things are always done at the last minute and in a rushed knee-jerk response. Meetings are frequently double booked and you end up at meetings where nothing actually seems to happen as a result. This will lead to stress and a feeling of going around in circles.

Look critically at your planner and the cycle of meetings; don't be afraid to cancel meetings if there is genuinely no need for them. Look also at how your meetings are structured and whether they are really effective meetings or simply opportunities for delivering information to your team (something that could be achieved on paper and does not have to be face to face). Look also at your procedures for discipline and ensure that matters are dealt with quickly and efficiently. Producing standard letters that could be issued to parents helps cut down on time wasting for both you and your team.

A major impact on your time management can be the temptation to help others do their work or to do the work of others in the belief that it is easier for you to do it rather than explain to someone else how you want it done. The art of delegation is essential to good time management, and so is trusting your team to deliver the goods once you have set them the task. Your experience of the skills and attributes of your team will allow you to set appropriate but nevertheless challenging tasks. This can ease your workload, provide opportunities for professional development of team members and engender a sense of ownership of the problems and solutions you all face as you strive to improve.

4

DEVELOPING ACTION PLANS

'The best laid schemes o' mice an' men
Gang aft a-gley'
To A Mouse – *Robert Burns*

This chapter explores the concept of action planning to effect school and departmental improvement. It looks at the process and stages involved in action planning and points out some of the pitfalls in implementing action plans. The issues of target setting, as a device for improvement and as a measure of success, will also be considered.

Year on year, many teacher-hours are taken up with action planning. If your school has recently been through an inspection process then you will already be constructing action plans as a result of the findings of the inspection. A regular agenda item in middle management and senior management meetings revolves around the issues arising from action planning and the school as a whole will have an overall development plan. There are many formats within which schools make and implement action plans and there is no one single right or wrong way of setting out the action plan. What has to be clear in the minds of everybody is the purpose of the action plan and how the process works. The Standards and Effectiveness Unit of the DfES has simple advice on the purposes and role of action planning in schools to help effect improvement. They state that good action planning:

❏ has a clear focus on raising attainment and promoting pupils' progress through concentrating, as appropriate, on the quality of teaching and learning;
❏ involves governors, parents, pupils and **all** staff in raising standards;
❏ complements and is integral to the school development plan; and
❏ contributes to the ongoing process of self evaluation and school improvement.

(DfEE, 1999)

Your first step is to see how action planning works in your school. If you have been involved in developing action plans and in the school development plan then you will have a pretty clear idea of the process and timing of the production of these plans. The cycle of planning, implementation review and evaluation (see Figure 4.1) will vary from school to school.

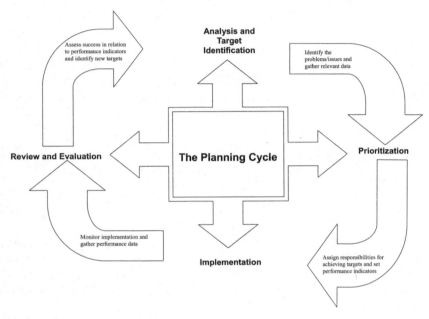

Figure 4.1 *The planning cycle*

Some like a fairly short cycle of perhaps two years, others take a longer view and can have a cycle that lasts up to five years. There are advantages and disadvantages with both. A short cycle leaves little time for effective implementation and a long cycle may be disrupted by a number of changes, such as staff leaving and joining or new initiatives from the DfES requiring immediate implementation. Most schools will, by now, have an established cycle for action and development planning. For many it is based around the OFSTED cycle of inspections that will normally occur on a four-year cycle. If you take over as a manager of a department or as a team leader, say in a head of year role, you will need to be aware of the phase of the planning cycle that you are in and what the latest action or development plan is. In addition, you will need information about the whole school development plan and the direction in which this is taking your area of responsibility.

DEVELOPMENT PLAN OR ACTION PLAN?

Two types of forward planning exist in many schools, the overall school development plan and the action plan. The development plan is normally a longer-term plan that sets out the direction in which the school is moving over, say, a five-year period. It will set out targets for progress and achievement and will focus not just on pupils but on staffing and the entire fabric of the school. It will consider the curriculum, the staffing structure, the targets for pupil progress and development, and set out the performance indicators that need to be achieved in order to satisfy the demands of the government, LEA, parents, pupils, staff and the governors of the school. All areas of the school, from academic to non-academic, from full-time to part-time staffing, and the involvement of outside bodies will be encompassed in a whole school development plan.

Action plans may be developed in response to a recent inspection and are required from schools to show how they will address any points arising from the inspection process. Action plans are also a common feature of curriculum and pastoral management in a school and require middle managers to say how they will respond not only to inspection demands but also to the whole school development plan. These action plans will set out how specific goals are to be achieved. Figure 4.2 shows the relationship between different development and action plans. This is a hypothetical relationship as the actual relationship may vary from school to school. At the centre of any action or development plan is a desire to raise achievement and progress as a school.

TARGET SETTING AND PRIORITIZATION

At the core of any development or action planning are target setting and prioritization. It is by striving to achieve specific targets, listed in order of priority, that the plan will succeed or fail. The relationship between the various plans that exist in schools is vital if the school is as a whole to move forward and progress towards higher standards of teaching and learning and pupil achievement. In Figure 4.2 you may notice that below the school level the relationship between the various plans is a two-way thing, but from the government and LEA things tend to be more of a one-way, top-down relationship. This is not wholly true as some aspects of school-based planning can be fed upwards and may have an effect on the development plans of LEAs and even governments, but this is limited in

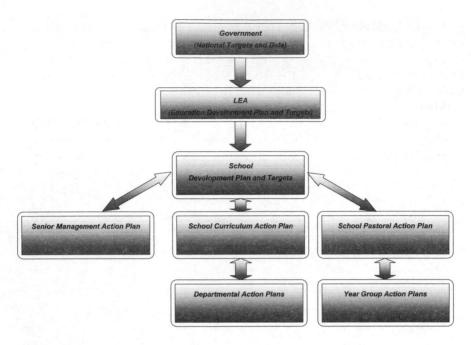

Figure 4.2 *Development and action plan relationships*

the extreme and so the relationship may really be regarded as almost always one-way. From the middle manager's point of view, plans that do exist in the school should be publicly available; indeed, modified and simplified plans should be available to the parents and other interested parties so that everyone understands what it is that the school as a whole is trying to achieve.

The work of the headteacher will, from time to time, be appraised by the governors, in much the same way as the work of all staff will be appraised. The status of the development and action plans will therefore have more importance as staff will be judged against their performance in achieving the targets set out in the various development and action plans. As Poster and Poster (1993) usefully point out, it is important to distinguish between the appraisal of staff against the development plans and the review and audit of the success of plans. They do note, however, that there is '... a symbiotic relationship between the two. The school development plan is the joint responsibility of all staff and in particular the headteacher, the governors and the LEA' (p 188). The use of development plans and action plans in appraisal must be restricted to illustrative use to show the general progress against agreed targets. The use of the development or action plan as a blunt instrument to beat around the head of individuals who fail to meet specific targets must be avoided. Many factors will influence the degree of success in achieving targets set out in development plans and those factors must be given due weight in assessing the work of staff and their contribution to the development plan as a whole.

When setting targets, the notion of challenging and achievable targets is often talked about. Many people find it difficult to set targets that fulfil these criteria. An approach that works well is to introduce the notion of stepped targets that can be both challenging and achievable. By stepping targets you eliminate the risk of staff (or pupils for that matter) looking at the target and giving up before they even begin, in the belief that the target is simply too hard to achieve. Consider the following notion for setting stepped targets.

Suppose that you wish to introduce targets for staff teaching various Key Stage 3 classes. Those targets may, perhaps, be based on the end of unit test results. If you were to set a blanket target of, say, an average 70 per cent result for the class for teacher A who takes set 1 and 60 per cent for teacher B who takes set 2, the teachers may return to you, stating that based on prior performance they feel that the targets are unrealistic. You are then faced with the situation of either convincing them that the target is realistic (a difficult proposition) or changing the target. Instead, consider the merits of setting stepped targets that allow the staff to realistically achieve one or two. As with pupils, when people make progress and achieve even small targets, their confidence is boosted and they often work harder and achieve more. So for teacher A you could set a baseline of 50 per cent that should be achieved with no real hardship for the teacher or the pupils. Then introduce steps of, say, 5 per cent with a top target of 70 per cent. You may even link the targets with a critique of your expectations, eg what you expect, what you would like as a top result and a level at which you feel that real progress is being made.

There are of course two dangers with target setting related to results, and with stepped targets. Firstly, results linked to internal tests and examinations may be 'fixed' by the teacher. Sometimes intentionally, sometimes not. The problems associated with lenient marking, giving pupils 'the benefit of the doubt' and inflating results may make the teacher appear to achieve targets that were thought to be challenging to say the least. With stepped targets there is a danger that members of staff will look at the steps and make a subconscious decision that they are willing to achieve and work towards, say, the second or third target but they will not carry on and try to achieve the top target.

A common criticism of action plans and school development plans it that they rarely achieve all that they set out to do. Should you look at your own school development plan from five years ago and audit how many of the targets have been achieved, let alone implemented in full, I suspect that many would not and could not legitimately be held to be actually in place. Many of the targets and actions may well be in place and to various degrees achieved, albeit in a modified form. The status of development plans and action plans within departments may be likened to transitional fossils in the evolutionary record. In fact development plans and action plans will only succeed if there is an element of evolutionary progress about them. Hard-and-fast plans are doomed to fail as they take little to no account of the changing environment in which they exist. In biology a basic tenet is that of evolution, and this provides a useful context within which to set development plans. The development of the theory of evolution by Alfred Russel Wallace and Charles Darwin rested on the notion of survival of the fittest. Those organisms that adapted and had features that suited the environment in which they existed survived, and those that were weak or that were unable to adapt died. This theory has since been refined many times, most notably with the notion of punctuated equilibrium and phyletic gradualism, as exemplified by Figure 4.3.

The implementation of various initiatives in education over the past 15 years mimics punctuated equilibrium. The introduction and development of the National Curriculum exemplifies the application of punctuated equilibrium, with periods of radical change followed by minor changes and periods of stability. The late 1980s saw a period of radical change as the National Curriculum was introduced. This was followed by minor changes until another radical change occurred with the publication of the Dearing Report and the production of the 1995 curriculum. This then heralded a five-year period of relative stability until the introduction of Curriculum 2000.

School development plans and departmental action plans have had to follow these changes and initiatives and so they have had to evolve to keep pace with the changing educational environment. Static plans are, like the unfit organisms of evolution, doomed to extinction. To follow plans rigidly without recourse to adjusting them in the light of the changing education environment is folly.

WHAT FACTORS MIGHT AFFECT THE EDUCATION ENVIRONMENT CHANGE?

Many things will affect how school development plans and action plans evolve. Each year the population of pupils will change with new pupils

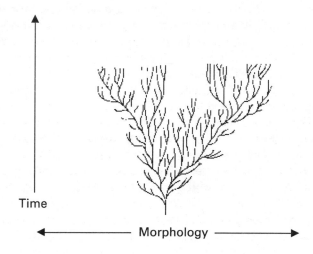

Phyletic gradualism, long slow changes over time

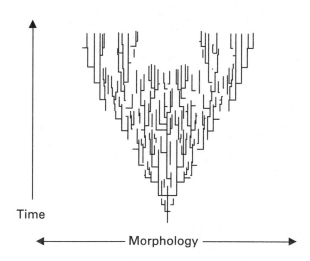

Punctuated equilibrium, periods of rapid change followed by long periods of no change

Figure 4.3

entering year 7. These pupils will have a different academic profile from their older peers and so may affect the targets set for academic achievement. This is lessened in schools that have a selection process and admit pupils on ability, though even then to a small degree the ability profile may change. The targets set may need to be reviewed up or down according to the new ability profile. This may be calculated by comparing the baseline assessment of Key Stage 2 results year on year.

Staffing changes may also have a large effect on development planning. As experienced staff leave, targets for which they may be wholly or partly responsible may need to be revised or responsibility for them allocated to other staff. We will consider staff job descriptions and strategies for dealing with reallocation of responsibilities in the chapter on staff selection and interviewing.

Any form of developmental planning must have associated with it a system of monitoring, review and evaluation. This is a four-stage process.

1. Specifying the purpose of the action plan item

You need to state in your action plan why this action item is needed and how it relates to the department in the first instance and to the whole school in the second.

The following questions should be asked:

❑ What do we hope to achieve by implementing this item from the development plan?
❑ At whom or at what is the item targeted? Pupils, staff, non-teaching staff, resources etc.
❑ What is the nature of the item? Is it related to teaching, learning, professional development, resources, etc?
❑ What is the timescale for the item to be effected?

2. Gathering the evidence

At this stage you must specify the evidence and how it is to be collected. Questions for this stage include:

❑ What documentary evidence can be used?
❑ What evidence is already available?
❑ Who is responsible for gathering the evidence?
❑ How will the evidence be gathered? For example, observation, survey, questionnaire, interviews etc.

3. Judging the evidence

For this stage you must have criteria upon which the evidence is to be judged. Some may call these criteria performance indicators. Whatever term is used, it must be agreed by the people involved in the implementation. If items relate to staff then it is vital that the staff know and understand the criteria against which judgements will be made.

Questions for this stage include:

❏ Are the criteria appropriate, valid and reliable?
❏ How have the criteria been devised? For example, against local or national norms, legal requirements.
❏ How will the findings be reported?
❏ To whom will the findings be reported?
❏ Who must have access to the findings and which parts of the report are they entitled to have access to? If it is a report on members of staff, then it is entirely appropriate that those same staff have access to that part of the report that concerns them, but it is not appropriate for them to have access to reports on their colleagues.
❏ Have you acted ethically and legally in obtaining the evidence and reporting on it?

4. Deciding on future action

As a result of the monitoring review and evaluation process, there will most probably be resulting actions that you wish to take. The following questions need consideration here:

❏ What action is needed in response to the findings?
❏ What effect would this action have on, for example, teaching, learning, effectiveness, efficiency etc?
❏ Do you have the resources and time to implement this action?
❏ Do you have the required skills?
❏ Is help from elsewhere appropriate in achieving this action?

5

TEAM BUILDING AND MOTIVATING

'Let's not do it your way or my way; let's do it the best way.'
Greg Anderson

This chapter explores the process of building a team that works together and the effects of changes in work practices and their effect on team development. It outlines the key elements of team building. The problems of taking over as a new manager in an established team will be looked at, and how cultural changes both within and between schools can occur and the effect on motivation. Influencing styles will be discussed and the basics of teamwork described.

Heads get hard lesson

New headteachers found themselves unexpectedly getting a taste of their own medicine as a US management guru gave them initial lessons in leadership. The lessons involved moving the back row to the front of the class, singing Beethoven's 'Ode to Joy' in German and singing 'Happy Birthday' to a poor head perched on a stool in front of the conference. The 'expert' was Ben Zander, founder of the Boston Phil, who uses his musical talents to improve management and leadership styles. Ministers and government advisers joined in the experiment at the conference, where Tony Blair had warned heads that they could expect better rewards for doing their job well but if they could not do it they faced the sack. The PM then unveiled plans for new training colleges for heads. The NUT said it was a pity the PM had to mar the occasion with yet another attack on teachers and heads.

Source: The Guardian, 21 October 1998, p 4

The article reproduced above is an example of what many think team building and motivational sessions are like in the business world. The notion of taking your team for a paint-balling session in the middle of nowhere to encourage greater team commitment or sending the team on a weekend survival course evokes images that we are all familiar with. But how do we greet such ideas in the school environment? Would you give up a weekend to spend time lashing together a raft of oil drums and planks in a cold, wet, wooded area with the boss saying 'we are all equal, just call me Bill and make no allowances'? In business this tactic was in vogue for much of the late 1980s and 90s. For some it worked. For many it mattered not one bit as the 'boss' often reverted to type once the weekend was over. Your problem as a middle manager will generally be one of two: 1) you take over a department or team and are perceived as an outsider with a hidden agenda; 2) you already lead a team that is not working at its best or are appointed from within the team to lead it.

In both of these situations the core problem is the same: how to build the team and motivate them to produce the best possible work. In other words, how do you move from the notion of a team to the experience of teamwork?

WHAT IS A TEAM?

Adair (1986) defines a team as a working group within which the contributions of individuals are seen as complementary. He goes on to state that an effective team depends on whether or not:

> Its members can work as a team while they are apart, contributing to a sequence of activities rather than to a common task, which requires their presence in one place and at one time.

In effect, teams are long-term work groups that display effective behaviours, which leads to task accomplishment and group satisfaction. McGregor (1960) described the differences between effective and ineffective groups. Table 5.1 lists the features as described by Cole (1996).

Groups can be found in any situation where two or more people interact. They may or may not have a common goal and purpose but they are likely to be working on the same or similar tasks. In many situations individuals will talk about teamwork and being a member of a team but they are, in reality, simply part of a group. In many instances newly appointed middle managers will actually take over a group rather than a team. If they are lucky enough to inherit a team it will still require them to exercise the basics

Table 5.1 *Characteristics of effective and ineffective groups (after Cole, 1996)*

EFFECTIVE GROUPS	INEFFECTIVE GROUPS
1. Informal, relaxed atmosphere	1. Boring or tense atmosphere
2. Relevant discussions	2. Discussion dominated by individuals or irrelevant
3. High degree of participation	3. Low degree of participation
4. Task or objective clear and understood	4. No clear task or objective
5. High degree of listening in group discussion	5. Low degree of listening in group discussion
6. Conflict dealt with objectively and fairly	6. Conflict is avoided or confrontational
7. Decisions reached by consensus	7. Decisions reached by simple majority vote with no consensus
8. Ideas expressed freely and openly	8. Ideas not forthcoming and reluctance to talk openly
9. Group is self governing and regularly reviews progress and behaviour	9. Group does not evaluate its performance
10. Leadership role for the completion of various tasks may be undertaken by group members	10. Leadership is always from the appointed group leader

of team building and motivation as they will have inherited someone else's team and will need to work to make the team their own.

THE FIRST STEPS

Regardless of whether you come from outside or from within to lead a team, the first stage is to find out about your team, to assess their skills, knowledge and understanding and to discover their potential. It is not dissimilar to what we do as teachers on a day-to-day basis; we assess prior knowledge and adjust our teaching to ensure that we challenge and stimulate the pupils into performing their best possible work as consistently as possible. It is exactly the same with a team, if not a little bit more sophisticated. Your team's greatest asset is their skills, knowledge and potential. The trick is to release these not just for the individual but for the team as a whole. In many schools, teams are not true teams with common goals and cooperative working practices. They are really just a collection or group of people, paying lip service to the notion of cooperative work. Many tales exist of staff-room loners and mavericks that, despite the best efforts of the management, fail to conform and rarely contribute to a team effort. Why does this happen? It goes back to habit in the first instance, often coupled with an insecurity about the notion of opening up to others the secrets of their working practices. True effective working teams share many similarities with families. There is often a sense of belonging, interdependence and a shared past. True team members will work closely together, often spending large amounts of time together. In many work situations the team will see more of each other in a working week than they will of their own family. It is important to realize that how well we work and function with others and how well we are treated by others are vital to an individual's success and personal satisfaction.

The first stage in team building requires an analysis of the constraints under which the team has to operate. There are four main considerations here:

❑   team size;
❑   the nature of the task;
❑   the environment within which the task is to be completed;
❑   the skills possessed by the team members.

Teams will vary in size from core subjects such as English, maths and science, where the team may be quite large, to smaller subjects in humanities where the team may consist of only two people. For heads of year the team size may not be the important factor but geographical distribution throughout the school may have an effect.

The task will change almost on a daily basis but overall there will be identified tasks that, as a team, need to be tackled. This may be anything from raising performance in a particular key stage, to looking at the evaluations of schemes of work, to assessing the impact of policy procedures put in place in a whole school context.

The environment may, as suggested earlier, be a major or minor consideration. For example, a team leader who is a head of year will have team members who may be spread through a number of departments in the school. Being specialists in different academic areas really presents few problems; however, being geographically located in different parts of the school may present problems for the team leader who needs to communicate with them frequently. By contrast, teams that may be geographically located together but who have to put up with inadequate accommodation or poorly resourced departments will also present the team leader with problems. The skills that teams have may also be diverse and some teams may consist entirely of relatively new staff or staff who have considerable experience and all shades between. For new middle managers, an added factor may be that some members of the team may have more experience in teaching than the manager. This creates other problems relating to communication and will be dealt with in Chapter 6.

THE TEAM CONCEPT

The senior management of the school will recognize that various teams are needed in order to meet its goals more efficiently and effectively. The teams will be set up and led by middle management, who should have identified the function of the team. In many cases the function is closely related to the vision of the headteacher, but will in any case be based on the raising of standards of teaching and learning. Sometimes the senior management will set up other teams that have specific functions, such as a curriculum team to look at the distribution of time across the curriculum or a team to look at a restructuring of the school day and produce a feasibility report. In this instance, however, we will look at the more long-term teambuilding process, rather than the short-term process involved in building teams for specific projects.

THE STAGES OF TEAM BUILDING

Assessing the resources

As has been mentioned, an assessment of the raw material for the team, ie the individual members, is the first step. It is also important to assess the raw materials available to the team members that will enable them to do the task in hand. If there are spaces in your team then you will need to seek new team members based upon their personal qualities and their technical expertise. At this point, careful consideration to job descriptions and advertisements for new staff must be a priority.

Curtis and Curtis (1997) identify two issues that face anyone who is tasked with any teambuilding role: individuality and self-interest. They state that in society, individuals seek to compete rather than work coopera-tively and so the notion of reward being based on individual achievement rather than being based on the outcome of a team effort is more common. This must be taken into account. Although the ultimate goal is a team, that team will, nevertheless, be made up of individuals. While the goal for achievement is a common understanding that all members of the team have to make a contribution to the achievement, people will have their own self-interests uppermost and will be looking carefully at the actual contributions of others.

In essence you will need to make a list of the skills of the individuals in your group and the resources available and match these to the problem the team has to solve. If there are weaknesses in the team, you must think how you are going to overcome this, eg specific INSET that addresses the weakness or allows one of the team members to acquire further skills.

Laying the foundations

Once the function of the team has been identified, the manager will need to plan carefully how the teambuilding process will operate. The team function may be explicit from the outset as the team may be a subject department or pastoral group, or it may be that this function needs to be identified, eg a curriculum sub-group or working party. In either case you will have recourse to look at the raw materials before the foundations can be properly laid. It is analogous to building a house. If the house, or task, is too big and the resources deficient, either in building materials or the skills needed to complete the building, then what results is an inadequate house that constantly needs attention, repairs and patching up. If the foundations are properly laid and the correct resources and skills are available, then what should result is a sturdy building capable of fulfilling its intended function for many years.

The success of the team will depend on this stage. All team members will need to be aware of their specific role and responsibility and be certain about what they are to contribute. The team also needs to know that they are performing for each other as well as for themselves and that failure will seek out the weakest link. Being aware of the needs of the individual as well as the needs of the team, the manager should also describe the benefits to the individuals in performing their task.

In the following hypothetical example the team manager will have assessed the members of their team and delegated one of them to rewrite the scheme of work for a series of units of work to incorporate references to literacy activities in line with the new whole school policy on literacy.

The benefits here for the team are obvious: all members will have reference to literacy that they can take account of in their lesson planning, but what of the benefit to the individuals? It could be twofold. The teachers may well increase their knowledge of literacy and thereby improve their teaching, or they may be able to use the opportunity to complete a module for a Master's degree they are undertaking on the application of the government literacy strategy in secondary schools. In this fictitious case you may well have identified that teacher's interest in the subject and their need to complete work for a higher degree before deciding on the best person to complete the task.

Team growth

Once tasks have been delegated to team members the team will grow mostly of its own accord. If your analysis of the team and task and the delegation of jobs are correct, the team should grow to perform together for a common purpose. At this stage your input to the team as a manager need only be a light touch. During the growth stage, four separate development phases have been identified through research (Tuckman, 1965).

Phase 1   Forming

If team members are new to each other or if there is a newcomer, the team will get to know each other. You may facilitate this by introducing team members, or by asking for cooperative work between two members of the group. If you are the new member of the team then the rest of the team will need to get to know you. This may be accomplished on two levels, on a private level, in social settings, or on a professional level as the team gets to know about the way in which new team members work.

Phase 2   Storming

This is often characterized by a period of conflict. There will be disagreements between team members and there will be times when the task seems doomed to fail as team members reveal their true feelings about either their delegated tasks or the tasks being undertaken by others. This is an important stage and, if negotiated successfully, will lead to a better team understanding and closer working relationships. The key point to remember is that this phase can rarely be avoided totally, but can lead to greater trust between team members if successfully negotiated.

As the team leader, you may have to take on a modifying/clarifying role. The tasks delegated to individuals might need redefining and procedures put in place for the completion of tasks might need modifying. What you cannot do is simply let conflict happen without any sense of you taking charge. It is easy in this situation for dominant team members to take over and assume control of the task. This must not be allowed to happen. If the leader loses control then the team may disintegrate and the task may never be achieved satisfactorily. The leader here must ensure that all of the participants in the group are able to contribute.

Phase 3   Norming

If phase two has been negotiated successfully there comes a period of calm where the group should begin to act as a cohesive force. Any problems will have been successfully dealt with and personality clashes and hostility to either others in the group or the task will have been tackled.

As a leader you can now afford to take less of a managing and leadership role and take on the work of one of the team. Hopefully the team will now be able to accept responsibility for the work and the task, though it is wise to ensure that this is being accomplished. If you feel, as a leader and manager, that the group is losing direction, then it may be appropriate to assume a leadership role again to ensure that the team is put back on the rails and steered towards the desired outcome.

Phase 4   Performing

In the final stage in group growth, the group should really be operating as a cohesive unit and be able to voice concerns and feelings without concern. It will be evident from the amount of work and the high quality of the work that the group is effective. Reaching this stage is the real goal of the manager. Exactly how long this may take will depend on a number of factors, not least the size of the group and the task set. In truth some teams will never reach this stage. This may be because of the ever-changing face of education making tasks overlap and priorities may reassign the focus for the group. Staff turnover may also disrupt the team and not allow all four stages to be achieved.

As the leader and manager of the team, less support is needed for teams in this phase. The amount of support should also be less, as will the need to direct the team towards the desired outcome. At this point the leader may well find that he or she can easily move on to address other tasks.

Phase 5   Adjourning

If a task is complete then the team may no longer be required to work on the problem. At this point the team may be disbanded. In a working party or committee set up to address a specific issue, the team members may return to other teams to carry on work in other areas and may not meet as a team again. In schools this is unlikely, due to the close relationship that often exists between staff members. It is vital, if a team is to be adjourned or disbanded, that there is some form of closure on the task. Recognition of the work of the team is vital to establishing and building confidence between the managers and others. Adjourning a team with no recognition of their work and no reference to the outcomes is a sure-fire way of demotivating people.

TEAM ROLES

If you sit and watch a team working, even if it is group work in pupils, you will see some team roles developing. Belbin (1981) describes eight team roles, and members of any team may fall into one or more role.

Chairman

This is a person who is neither threatened nor impressed by others in the team. This person can effectively deploy team members to ensure that they fulfil their potential. The chairman type will not show a great deal of imagination and is mostly concerned about what is possible and is not given to being easily excited. They often lack imagination

Innovator

Unlike the chairman, this team member is the creative type. The idea, should it be a good one, will often take precedence over the feelings of others.

Shaper

Shapers are constantly directing the work of others. They will often set priorities and objectives and try to ensure that the team is set to work meeting the objectives in the correct order of priorities. They often remind others of the objectives and priorities at meetings if they feel that the group is moving off at a tangent.

Resource investigator

These are the researchers who like nothing better than to look outside the team for ideas and resources to support the work of others. They are often the people who contribute to meetings by stating that they know of something that could help the team achieve its objectives or, if they do not know, will offer their services as a 'finder', looking for examples, resources and ideas for the team.

Team worker

This type will often support others in their attempts to move from an initial idea to a completed project. They are collaborative workers and aid cohesiveness in teams. These people are often very perceptive of the needs of others and frequently offer time and their own resources to enable others to complete tasks.

Company worker

The company worker exists for the company, or in our case, the good of the school. They are loyal to the school and its management and are the type that will translate general ideas into actual practice. If the Head says that there is to be a crackdown on wearing coats in school, then the first to jump into action is invariably the company worker.

Monitor

The monitor is good at analysis and will be able, in meetings, to offer succinct analyses of the progress and outcomes of any task that the team is undertaking. During the initial discussions on tasks, they are often the people that can offer objective analysis of what is required and what the problems may be.

Completer

Completers are good at the detail; they pay attention to the detail when others may be looking at the whole task. The problem is that the detail can often bog down completers. Although they are intent on completing a task and often feel unfulfilled when tasks or aspects of the task remain incomplete, they are useful in working towards getting the job done on time and to an acceptable standard.

You will need to know the characteristics of your team and how they fit into Belbin's roles. People do not, except in exceptional circumstances, fit into one role all the time. In practice, people will assume aspects of two or more of these roles dependent on the task, their expertise and the peer group that they are operating in at any one time. Just as a class can change its characteristics from day to day and from peer group mix to peer group mix, so too will the team. If the company worker is missing from a meeting or series of meetings then their role may be taken over by others who recognize that an element normally present is missing. As a leader and manager you will need to be aware of the positive and negative aspects of each of these team roles when managing your meetings. You will also need to take on roles as and when required to ensure that the balance of the team is right.

After reading the roles described above, how would you characterize yourself and your colleagues? What sort of mix do you have in your department? A key factor to team building and motivation is knowing the predominant characteristic of each of your team members and working with them to harness their strengths. It is also important for their own professional development to experience other styles and to become flexible in their role in a team.

MOTIVATING YOUR TEAM

What motivates you? If you sit down and analyse your motivation for doing something, you will find that there are many and varied reasons why you were motivated to do something:

❑   for personal satisfaction;
❑   to help others;
❑   for personal gain;
❑   to improve the working/living conditions of others;

❏ from a sense of loyalty;
❏ for religious purposes.

The list can be exhaustive and will vary from person to person. In education the vocational element to the job is often put up as a motivating factor for being a teacher. As an interviewer of prospective teachers, the issue of motivation can often throw up some interesting situations. Some prospective students are motivated by the notion of helping young people to further themselves. Others are motivated to teach because of the love of their subject. Rarely during an interview does money play an important part in motivating people to become a teacher. Yet the increase in applications for teaching once financial incentives were announced could be interpreted as a motivational factor. It may also be simply that it allowed people who otherwise could not afford to enter teaching to give up employment for a period of time to train. In business, money can be a great motivator when there are bonuses and incentive payments to be made for productivity. Although appraisal has now entered teaching and the massive 80 per cent uptake for the first round of threshold performance applications might point towards money as a motivational factor, it can never be as prominent as it is in industry. So just how do you motivate teachers, given that offering huge bonuses is neither practical nor desirable in an educational setting?

The universal motivator for people in general, and not just teachers, is recognition of their work and performance. The recognition may go under the banner of performance pay but in reality the key factor is recognition of the hard work undertaken by teachers everyday. As a manager and leader, that recognition must start with you. By genuinely recognizing the work of others in your team you will motivate them to do better and reward them for their efforts. Drawing the line between genuine recognition and patronizing platitudes is difficult. If you walk around all day saying 'well done team, excellent job, keep up the good work etc', the effect will soon wear off, especially if the praise is recognized as false.

Some time ago, while observing a trainee teacher, it was clear that she had been told to praise the pupils and that positive reinforcement was a good thing. The problem occurred when she simply praised without really checking that the work was worthy of praise. Pupils soon caught on that no matter what they did she would at some point invariably walk around the room uttering empty phrases to whoever caught her eye. The praise was empty and she began to lose their respect. As a precursor to praise, check that the work merits the praise.

Maslow's Hierarchy of Needs and Herzberg's Motivation-Hygiene Theory

Maslow (1987) described specific groups of needs that most people subscribe to:

1. self-fulfilment;
2. self-esteem;
3. affection;
4. safety;
5. physiological.

The first three are higher-order needs and the final two are lower-order needs. Maslow states that people tend to move from the lower-order needs, satisfying these first, and then on to the higher-order needs. Maslow also argued that each group of needs has to be satisfied before the move to the next hierarchical order is effected. His argument ran along the lines that a hungry person will not care about safety, affection, self-esteem or self-fulfilment until the hunger is satisfied. Another analysis of motivation carried out by Herzberg (1959) was developed into a motivation-hygiene theory. In this study engineers were asked to recall aspects of their job that led to satisfaction (motivation) and dissatisfaction (hygiene). The results of this study led to the description of motivators and demotivators (see Table 5.2). Herzberg concluded that most if not all of the motivators were related to the type of work and what actually had to be done, ie the content, whereas the demotivators were mainly about the environment in which the work had to be carried out.

If you have ever wondered how certain people can, for example, enjoy their working life in a sewer, then Herzberg's theory can explain that the motivation, ie the content of the job and what the worker is achieving, is far outweighing the environment of the job, ie the sewer.

Table 5.2 *Motivational/Demotivational factors*

MOTIVATORS	DEMOTIVATORS
Achievement	School policy
Recognition	Supervision
The work itself	Salary
Responsibility	Interpersonal relations
Advancement	Working conditions

A key point to remember in motivation is that Herzberg's hygiene factors cannot in themselves lead to job satisfaction; they can only prevent dissatisfaction from occurring. If there are no motivators, or insufficient motivators, then no matter how pleasant the environment, the lack of challenge in the content of the job will still lead to dissatisfaction. There are also exceptions to this in that a person's salary can of course be linked to satisfaction; being paid a large salary may go some of the way to compensating for difficult conditions, but even this cannot in the long run provide motivation if it is the sole compensator. Figure 5.1 graphically shows the factors and the probable overlap from dissatisfaction to satisfaction.

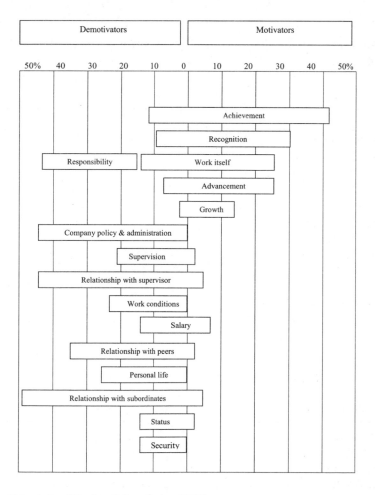

Figure 5.1 *Job attitudes (after Cole, 1996)*

Theory X and Theory Y

How we view others was the subject of work carried out by McGregor (1960). He looked at how managers categorize workers. From this he developed Theory X and Theory Y. Theory X states that managers assume that the workforce does not in fact want to work. Theory Y states that managers assume that people actually enjoy their work. In developing these two extremes, McGregor made assumptions. For Theory X the assumptions are that people have an inherent dislike of work and that they will, at every available opportunity, avoid working if at all possible. As a result, managers believe that workers that fit Theory X need to be coerced, controlled, directed and threatened in order to achieve. In principle, Theory X people do not object to this as they need direction and enjoy the security of being reliant on others. They will often do the job and, if criticized, rely on the fact that they have been directed to do the job in this way and cannot therefore be criticized for it by others.

Theory Y assumptions are that workers will put everything into the job, expending as much time and energy as is necessary to complete the job. They will put as much into the job as they would their favourite hobby or pastime. In this case Theory Y people will be self-motivational, self-directed and committed to the job. Theory Y people will seek responsibility and accept it readily. Imagination and creativity are also high on the skills list of Theory Y people.

There is no doubting that team building and motivation come high on the list of priorities for the middle manager. However, it is the responsibility of all managers, from the senior management down, to create the environment where teams can work most effectively. As Herzberg's Motivation-Hygiene theory shows, the hygiene factors (the working environment) may not lead to complete satisfaction but they can override other factors and contribute to dissatisfaction. If meetings are all about the negative side of environmental factors, such as ineffective or trivial policies, poor working conditions, poor status and excessive burdens on administration, then there has to be a sea change in the working environment before the move from a dissatisfied team to a satisfied team can take place.

The process of team building cannot be achieved effectively if the team is dissatisfied. There is a chicken and egg situation here. What comes first, the team or the motivation? The answer, unlike the chicken and egg conundrum, has to be tempered with those things that you can control. If there are environmental or hygiene factors that you can control and make acceptable to the team, then that must be a priority before the team building begins. If you do effect any changes in working conditions or practices it will be a means to improving relationships and building trust. On this the first steps of teamwork can be built. If there is no effective control over work conditions and practices, then the team building must begin and you must concentrate on tasks that may help to improve the working environment.

6

EFFECTIVE COMMUNICATION

*'Some persons talk simply because they think sound is
more manageable than silence.'*
Margaret Halsey (1910–), US author

To be an effective communicator simply means to have your message understood by everybody. Unfortunately, many times messages sent out by leaders and managers are misinterpreted and misunderstood. Often we are not aware that misunderstanding and misinterpretation have taken place until we wonder why something has not happened or has not been carried out in the way that we wished it to be. So what is it that actually characterizes our messages and what are the factors that lead to effective communication? If we ask people how to make things clear or how to make our intentions clear, most would reply that we should choose our words carefully. This is not bad advice, but when we consider that the words we actually use account for less than 10 per cent of things that people use to help them interpret meaning from our messages, we must look to other factors. About 55 per cent of meaning is apparently derived from our posture, expression and our breathing pattern. Another 38 per cent is derived from the pitch, tone and quality of the voice, and the rest comes from the actual words we use.

If we are to communicate effectively we must understand how all of these elements work together to provide meaning and then we must be aware of how we convey meaning in the words and the manner in which we use them in different situations. Communication, however, is not just about words and how we use them in meetings or in presentations. There is also written communication and the way in which we lead or manage by example.

WHISPERS

There are many examples of 'whispers', taking a circle of people and instigating a message by whispering it into the ear of your neighbour, who communicates the message by whispering his or her interpretation to his or her neighbour and so on until the message comes back to the originator. At that point the fun of the game is to compare the original message with the returned message. Often the message is completely twisted and a new, sometimes entirely different meaning results. This is, of course, ineffective communication. But it is surprising how many messages in schools are misunderstood and misinterpreted. There are some key elements to effective communication that are easily mastered.

THE KEY ELEMENTS OF INTERPERSONAL COMMUNICATION

It is obvious that vocal skills, visual elements, personality and openness are the primary ingredients of high-level interpersonal skills. Effective communication can be summed up in nine behavioural skills, all of which can be learnt, though many come naturally to good managers and leaders:

1. *Eye communication.* In individual communication, eye contact should range between 5 and 15 seconds. If it is in a group situation, then about 4 seconds for an individual is recommended. Look for too long and the person becomes uncomfortable (that is why teachers demand eye contact with pupils, as it makes them uncomfortable!), don't give any eye contact and people will wonder what it is you have to hide.
2. *Posture and movement.* Stand tall and try to move naturally and easily. When trying to communicate, try not to get locked into a rigid position. Moving around all the time is distracting, but a rigid stance looks as if you are tense, stressed and not comfortable delivering the news.
3. *Gestures and facial movements.* Learn to be relaxed and natural when you speak. Relax your arms and hands at your sides. Gestures are fine provided they are not exaggerated and over the top. Facially you should try to learn to smile, especially when under pressure, as this conveys the opposite to what you are really feeling. It is the duck manoeuvre. Appear calm on the surface whilst paddling like hell under the water to maintain your position.

4. *Dress and appearance.* Dress, groom and appear appropriate for the environment you are in. How much less respect would you have for your headteacher's authority if he or she turned up in a stained T-shirt and wearing slippers?

5. *Voice and vocal variety.* Learn to know the sound of your own voice. If you can bear it, record yourself in real situations to hear how you sound to others. Just like teaching, a boring teacher often has a boring voice. As teachers, we are actors and the tool of the actor is voice. Try not to go to the 'radio voice', as this has to convey the meaning that we take for granted when we see someone. Practise varying the pitch, tone and intensity of the voice to suit different situations.

6. *Language, pauses and no words.* Language *is* the ultimate communicator. We have a rich language with many words. This is an asset and a problem. Having so many words and so many synonyms and antonyms can obfuscate communication; in other words, there are so many words with the same meaning it can make communication difficult or interesting. By 'interesting' I mean: Stimulating; Attractive; Sparkling; Piquant; Enticing; Exciting. Get the drift?

   Do not be afraid to pause. A pause in the right place can be very effective.

7. *Listener involvement.* Maintain the active interest and involvement of others whenever you speak. They must be drawn in to what you are saying or discussing, otherwise it can lead to them switching off and not taking in the important points you want to make. Always look at the faces of your audience, be it one person or one thousand people. They must be involved and be seen to be involved. You can grab attention using some simple ploys, like a direct question if you wish to be blunt, or a change in pace, volume or emphasis if you wish to be subtle.

8. *Use humour.* You can create a bond between yourself and your listeners through the use of humour. This means that they will enjoy listening to you and become engaged with the subject matter. There are a few simple rules: 1) don't tell jokes, that's the job of the stand-up comedian; 2) do tell stories and anecdotes, but craft them to a suitable length.

9. *Be your natural self.* Unless you are a very good actor you will not be able to create a persona and keep it up for long. Pretending to be something else or trying to fool your department into believing that you are a mystery man or woman with an unknown past will almost certainly fail. You will need to give of yourself, but you can still draw boundaries over which you may choose not to cross.

Decker (1988) states that the key ingredient to effective communication is credibility. How credible you appear to be when you speak to colleagues is difficult to assess. It is clear that the tone of voice used must convey sincerity and credibility and not convey a patronizing tone. Treating all staff as equals goes a long way to dispelling a patronizing tone.

In meetings you must be businesslike but not appear arrogant or flippant. Often your department or team will want to know whether or not you agree with 'us' or 'them'. Often, provocative comments are deliberately made by staff to see what your reaction is. Do you join in with the condemnation of the latest senior management team wheeze or do you appear to support it? Your team will be looking for verbal and visual clues. They will be doing this subconsciously, listening carefully to what you say and how you say it, along with an assessment of your body language. Are you, for example, being defensive? Are you pulling away from the people you are facing, sitting with your arms crossed? All of these give us visual clues as to what the other person is thinking and what their true feelings are towards a subject.

ORGANIZATIONAL COMMUNICATION

As well as effective personal communication, there is also a need to establish effective communication chains both within the department and across the school. The organization of communication within the department will largely be down to you as the head of department or subject leader. The school will already have a whole school approach to communication, or a communications protocol: assemblies to communicate to pupils; news-letters, meetings etc to communicate to parents; and meetings, briefings and memos etc to communicate to staff. The four overriding questions facing anyone thinking of setting up a communications protocol are:

❏ What needs to be communicated?
❏ How should communications be made?
❏ With whom are we communicating?
❏ How should communication take place?

When considering these four questions, the direction of communication must be borne in mind. Information, in whatever form, does not simply leave one place and end up in another without direction being imparted. There are three possible directions for the information to travel: upwards, downwards and laterally. In some cases you will be the originator of the information and you will determine the direction of the information; in other cases you will be the agent of communication and the direction will have been decided by others. Whatever the case, you will be part of a communications network that distributes the information.

COMMUNICATIONS NETWORKS

Cole (1996) describes a number of communications networks and categorizes five types of network: chain, wheel, circle, Y and all-channel (see Figure 6.1). Cole describes those networks that are centralized, characterized by the wheel, and those that are decentralized, the circle and all-channel. The chain and Y networks are in effect hierarchical networks. Which network you use, or which network is in operation at your school, may indicate leadership preference, with the Y and chain networks having a clear chain of command and message directions that are upward and downward only. The centralized wheel network will also have a clear leader, at the centre of the network, but it will allow for lateral communication in a way that the other two networks do not. Only the circle and all-channel networks provide for shared leadership and multidirectional communication, with an emphasis on the lateral. Cole indicates that organizations that have a mechanistic approach tend to rely heavily on the chain, Y and wheel networks. It is common in schools to find these networks, and relatively uncommon to find circle and all-channel networks.

There is a tendency in many organizations, and in schools in particular, to rely on a vertical communications network. The governors and senior management team will often convey their vision, policies, procedures, development plans and instructions through a chain to the workforce. This is a predominantly downward communication strategy and relies on a clear line of management through which the message is conveyed. Less common, though still valid, is the upward communication from staff to the senior management team and governors. More often than not, this upward communication is either in response to an earlier downward communication asking for feedback on certain issues and ideas/procedures, or in some cases conveying a grievance from the staff or some section of the staff to senior managers.

How quickly or effectively the communications travel, either up or down the chain, Y or wheel, can often be determined by the originator of the communication. In the case of a message from the headteacher or deputy headteacher, there is an excellent chance that the original message will be directly communicated to all staff in the chain or wheel. In the case of a

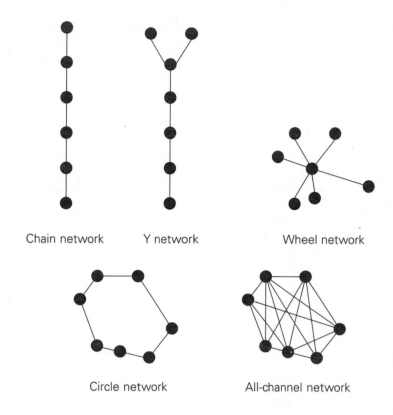

Chain network   Y network   Wheel network

Circle network   All-channel network

Figure 6.1 *Communication networks, after Cole (1996)*

grievance, there are often points in the chain where the issue will be dealt with without reference to a higher authority. This is not an attempt to limit access to the higher echelons of the management team but a genuine attempt to restrict the demands on the time of the most senior managers. The size of the organization also plays an important role here. In a small school setting with relatively few staff and a small cohort of pupils, the demands on the time of senior managers, while still high, are not as comprehensive as the demands on the headteacher of a 1,500-pupil split-site secondary school. In these two cases, getting to see the person at the top and getting your grievance aired is relatively easier in scenario 1 than seeing the headteacher of scenario 2. The dominant force in vertical communication networks is therefore downward communication.

Lateral communication is a more effective way of communicating policies, ideas and information but the mechanisms can be time consuming for middle managers and senior managers. Lateral communication is usually effected by interdepartmental meetings, the setting up of working parties or sub-committees. The problem for managers at all levels is that you may be involved in more than one area of the school and will be required to attend many meetings. The Special Educational Needs Coordinator (SENCO) is in just such a position, having to serve the interests of all departments across the school on behalf of their pupils. The solution to this problem is not to attend all meetings but to devolve the role of SEN to nominated people within departments who are then, in turn, required to attend meetings run by the SENCO. The greater the lateral communication, the greater the degree of delegation from the senior managers. To achieve this degree of delegation requires clear statements of performance criteria and limits of responsibility. In schools, while tasks may be delegated, responsibility may not. It is therefore sometimes difficult to let go of the task, knowing that should things go wrong the responsibility still falls on your shoulders. One method that headteachers and other managers sometimes employ is to delegate the task but safeguard their position by insisting on full communication of all matters under discussion and always to be 'kept in the picture'. The problem with this strategy is that the sheer volume of information required negates the usefulness of the exercise, as the manager concerned simply will not have the time to devote to comprehensively digesting and acting on the information received. For this strategy of communication to work, there must be clear performance standards and fixed, if somewhat limited, responsibilities. The result of this will be that communication with senior managers can be kept to a minimum, with reports and digests of meetings and decisions and full details only disclosed during periodic reviews of the work and if a problem arises.

THE MEDIA OF COMMUNICATION

The 'how' of communication is determined by the media of communication. Memos, e-mails, reports, notices etc are the media that dominate education. Written communications are permanent records of communication, even scribbled notes on the backs of envelopes can be 'used in evidence', so care is needed in the wording of any written communication. If written with care, while there is a chance of misinterpretation, the message can be clearly communicated, and to a large number of people if necessary. The speed of written communication, though much faster today than 20 years ago, with the advent of the Internet, WWW and e-mail, is still slower than a quick conversation in the corridor or a telephone call to the staff member to ask for a task to be completed. The problem with new technology and faster communication is that more immediate responses are expected. While it is perfectly acceptable for a letter to take two or three days to arrive and for the response to take another two or three days, the fax screams at us to respond immediately. The e-mail begs to inform us that this is a high priority communication needing our priority attention. Follow-up faxes and e-mail seem to come at an unhealthily fast pace, demanding our immediate attention.

Strategies that large organizations have adopted to deal with the fast communication demands include the automated reply of a standard 'holding' letter informing the originator that a more detailed and considered reply will be forthcoming ASAP. While this tactic can help in large organizations, a holding letter to the chair of governors, who is demanding information and a response to an issue or perhaps complaint, will neither satisfy nor be accepted. There is, however, a need for all managers, from the most junior to the most senior, not to jump into communications, especially if they may be of a sensitive nature, until all of the facts are clear and a considered response can be made. As a manager and leader, you will need to adopt a stance that respectfully declines to talk about serious and important issues until you can appraise yourself of the full facts and give a considered reply. One underhand tactic of management is to try to catch people 'off guard' where there is a problem or issue that needs their input and perhaps cooperation. Being railroaded into making decisions without having time and information to consider all implications is bad management. Railroading others into taking decisions in this fashion is weak defensive management.

While written communication is the preferred method, you will not get away from having to communicate orally with your staff, your line managers and others. Although more immediate and certainly the fastest communication method to small groups or individuals, the capacity for misinterpretation is much greater. Messages will rarely be remembered word for word and the problems of 'whispers' mentioned earlier is compounded by the slant placed on what is said by the listener, who may be keen to 'hear what they want to hear' and not what was actually said. This is especially true of telephone conversations. Next time you hold a telephone conversation, try writing down word for word who said what after you put the phone down. You will rarely be able to do this, though you will be able to give the gist of what was said. When dealing with any important issues by telephone, make notes during the conversation and date and time them so that you can, at a later date if required, provide objective evidence about who said what to whom.

You will at some point be asked to present reports to senior managers or outside agencies. Report writing is a skill that can be learnt. The structure

Table 6.1 *Common elements of a report and typical report structure*

FRONT PAGE	TITLE
	Author
	Date
Index	Headings and page numbers
	Subheadings and page numbers
Summary page	Bullet point main findings and conclusions
Main body	Introduction
	Description
	Findings
	Implications
	Conclusions
	Recommendations
Appendices	(As appropriate)

of reports is simple and straightforward. The party requesting the report may also specify the structure. A typical report has the structure outlined in Table 6.1.

Reports will also vary in length according to the subject of the report. Reports are useful devices for the evaluation phase of the developmental cycle. The key is to assemble your data and information in a logical format that presents, as clearly as you can, the key facts and arguments surrounding the issue in question. The length of the report is not the key factor; the conciseness and clarity of the report are the things to concentrate on.

In addition to reports, you may also be asked to make a presentation to the management team, governors, parents etc. Most often a presentation is about selling an idea, a concept, a strategy etc. As such, a presentation requires different skills and a different structure from a report. Many people make use of presentation software to help them organize their thoughts and to produce a bulleted set of transparencies. Whether yours is a high-tech computer-generated and projected presentation or a handwritten set of transparencies, there are some key things to remember when making presentations, summed up by the three Ps:

❏ Prepare
❏ Produce
❏ Present

Prepare

When preparing for a presentation, you must consider the content and how you are going to deliver it. The content is the most crucial factor. In many cases you will have too much content rather than too little. Each aspect of the content must be able to justify its place within your presentation. Decide what to keep in and what to leave out. You will most likely have a specific time slot within which your presentation must be completed. Make sure that only the key important facts are included and not the peripheral.

Produce

When producing the transparencies or notes, make sure that they are legible and presented to as high a standard as possible. Where possible use presentation software to help you. Do not overfill the transparencies or produce ineffective ones that people will be unable to read. Nothing irritates more than a presenter putting up a transparency, declaring to their audience that it is illegible and then proceeding to read out what is on the sheet. Each transparency or set of notes must clearly be sign-posted so that people can find their place. If something has to be included that makes an illegible transparency, summarize it in a few bullet points and include the full document in a set of handouts. A common complaint that people have during presentations is a lack of time or opportunity to copy down what is on the transparency. Make life as easy as you can for your audience by producing a set of notes that include all of the information on the transparencies. People are then free to make additional notes about your commentary and free to actually listen to your presentation rather than concentrate on writing down what you are showing them.

Present

Do not read the bullet points out; talk to them and around them. People can (if the transparencies are produced well) read for themselves. Be enthusiastic about the subject matter, but also be aware of its likely impact. Telling staff about budget cuts and possible redundancies cannot and must not be done with glee, relish and abundant enthusiasm. Be as natural a presenter as you can; above all else, remember that this is not a lesson and that the audience is not made up of children. If you forget this, your presentation will be regarded as highly patronizing and do you no favours as a manager.

OBSTACLES TO EFFECTIVE COMMUNICATION

There are a number of reasons why communications will meet obstacles. Some may be as a result of how you choose to communicate, what is being communicated or, more frequently, the response of the person or persons to whom you are communicating.

People will hear what they want to hear, see what they want to see and read what they want to read. This bias is to some extent in us all and we must work to overcome it. People will have developed their own value-systems and these may be connected with their background, beliefs (religious or otherwise) and prior experiences. Sometimes they will be unaware of this and as a manager you will have to bring it to their attention and discuss any possible bias to ensure that what is being communicated is taken without any bias.

Often a mistrust of managers, especially senior managers, will prove to be a big obstacle. Again this is tempered by a person's prior experiences: have they been let down in the past or have they a genuine reason to mistrust the messenger? Added to this can be a fear factor, sometimes fear of the unknown, sometimes an irrational fear of what may happen as a result of a change in working conditions, for example. This can be compounded by the person delivering bad news. No one relishes giving bad news to their colleagues. In an attempt to soften the blow we can make the mistake of only delivering part of the message. We may leave out information which may, at a later date, come into the open, resulting in a worsening of the situation. The fears that people have of the unknown are real, and keeping back information will not help them, however much you think it will. It is far better to be open, honest, impartial and, most importantly, supportive if the information you have to communicate is bad. In most cases the delivery of bad news will not come as a surprise to the person or persons involved. We are all aware of the school grapevine and how effective and extensive it can be. Be prepared to deliver the news by fully appraising yourself of its content, message and, most importantly, implications. Do not jump straight into the bad news, but do not take forever to get to the point of the message. Give a brief synopsis of the situation and bullet the relevant points. Then deliver the message. It is helpful if, beforehand, you carefully write down what you are going to say and then objectively look at what you are saying and how the team (person) may react or interpret. Give people time to consider what you have said and be prepared for a range of reactions and emotions. Above all, do not put up a barrier and refuse to listen to or discuss the responses, arguments and problems raised by the person(s) involved. It may well be that you are simply the messenger and that you are under instruction to deliver the bad news. This does not mean that you can simply wash your hands of it and pass the buck. You will have to be as supportive as you can and, if necessary, agree to become the mediator between the originator and recipient of the message. Offer constructive advice where possible and, if it is a very serious issue, such as a failing teacher, remember to advise them to seek help and advice from an independent source, such as a union.

You must not overlook your position in the hierarchy of the school management system. You have been granted certain power and authority over the running of the staff and the day-to-day running of the department. Sometimes an off-the-cuff remark by you, intended no more as a criticism than merely an observation, will have meaning attached to it that was never intended. The singer and songwriter Don McClean was once asked in an interview what the song 'American Pie' really meant to him. After a short break and sharp intake of breath, he replied that it meant that he never had to work another day in his life if he didn't want to. This was not the response the interviewer hoped for but it was, nevertheless, a deliberate ploy by the singer to avoid trying to explain if there really was any deep philosophical meaning to one of America's most popular songs. Academics argue over meaning, philosophers wax lyrical about meaning, but sometimes there is no meaning other than the simple translation of the words spoken. It is a simple fact that the higher up the ladder of management you climb, the more meaning there is attached to your simplest phrases.

The use of jargon and genuine language barriers may also prove to be obstacles to clear communication. Think carefully about introducing jargon. Many people would rather sit in ignorance of the literal translation of jargon than own up to the fact that they do not know what it means. Use the rule of thumb that journalists use. If you are going to use an acronym, the first time it is used write it (say it) in full and then use the acronym.

A final obstacle to effective communication is communication overload. When there is too much information, people will simply give up and not persevere with the mound of paper they have been given or the long, complex instructions issued. In the report structure is the most useful device that a manager can have, the executive summary. When you are inundated by the latest communications from the DfES and the many other organizations that have input into twenty-first-century education, go straight for the executive summary. It should contain all of the bullet points that you will need in order to get a grip on the document as a whole. Provide this service for your staff, produce the summary for them and do not simply copy the whole thing. When an issue arises that needs more detail or clarification, then is the time to delve into the body of the communication.

We live in an information-dominated society and our problem is one of too much information rather than a lack of information. While technology such as the Internet and WWW has transformed the sharing of knowledge, it has also led to another problem, information overload. Many circulars, guidance notes, lesson plans and useful research exists on the Web. There is also much misinformation and, frankly, rubbish. As a manager you have a responsibility to direct people towards information, good information and useful information. You cannot have the responsibility of making them read that information; that is their responsibility.

7

MANAGING MEETINGS

*'Soufflé is more important than you think. If men ate soufflé
before meetings, life could be much different.'*
Jacques Baeyens, French consul general, 1958

For most teachers, meetings are an intrusion into the working day. More often than not, in an analysis of time spent at meetings and INSET days, teachers find themselves stating that their time is being wasted. They feel that they would be far better off being left to their own devices doing 'more important' or pressing work such as marking, moderating or catching up on other forms of paperwork. For meetings to be successful there must be a feeling that something was accomplished as a result of meeting together. It may sound very simplistic to say this, but much of the frustration of meetings revolves around the feeling that the meeting accomplished nothing, that no decisions were made.

Campbell and Neill (1997) analysed teachers' time and found that on average teachers spent 2.5 hours per week at meetings. As a department head or subject leader you will inevitably find yourself at meetings for a longer period than this. It is important that you have an effective strategy for running meetings so staff feel that meetings are themselves effective. Campbell and Neill (1997) also described a profile of secondary teachers' work, breaking their job into 27 subcategories. As you would expect, teaching, planning and preparation take up the most time, 29.8 hours, with another 18.1 hours spent on administration. Only 5.3 hours were spent on professional development (INSET, meetings etc) and 4.1 hours on other activities (clubs etc). This amounts to an average working week of 57.3 hours. This is far in excess of the demands of other professional jobs.

Meetings themselves take up less time than we may imagine, though the pressures of new initiatives have probably increased the time spent at meetings for many teachers. Administration as a whole takes up the greatest amount of a teacher's week (18.1 hours). The government's promise of an independent review of teachers' workloads must look carefully at the time

ion and low-grade clerical work as compared to
reparation. It has been a long-held contention of mine
se standards in schools and to raise results and have
ng is not to increase testing (the government's current
regime) but to ~~~~~ achers to teach less and to prepare more. As a teacher
trainer I always advocate meticulous planning as the key to a good lesson.
If all teachers were allowed more freedom from the administrative burden
to spend more time planning and marking, standards would inevitably
rise. This would be a costly course for the government, however, and one
that would not prove easy to implement given the current problems with
trainee teacher recruitment.

EFFECTIVE MEETINGS STRATEGY

Guideline 1   Follow the agenda

Too often attendees enter a meeting unaware of what the meeting is about.
When they don't know what to expect they will not know how to prepare
for the issues that may arise. Key facts, data and information may be missing
or left behind and this can result in wasted time.

Publish the agenda as far in advance as possible and ask for items of
any other business to be submitted by a certain point. Include these items
in an agenda update the day before the meeting is due. Do not accept last-
minute items for Any Other Business (AOB) and most certainly do not
accept them after the meeting has started. Some people see AOB as their
opportunity to hijack a meeting and impose their own thoughts and views
on a particular subject. If an item of AOB is going to be controversial, you
will need time to think about the best approach to take during the meeting.
You may even be able to discuss the issue with the proposer and resolve it
without having to resort to including it in a meeting agenda.

List a start and end time for the meeting and try to allocate discussion
time for each agenda item. If an agenda item can be dealt with as a paper
issued to the department, issue the paper and ask for comment, but do not
simply read out what is in the paper.

Guideline 2   List outcomes, not subjects

When writing the minutes of the meeting, a short description of the subject
and a brief discussion of what was said and by whom is useful, but at the
end of the day the important fact is what was decided and what is to be

done and by whom. Minutes should accurately reflect what was said at the meeting and should not be written with bias. For this reason it is important that the chair of the meeting does not write the minutes. You cannot effectively chair a meeting and keep order and time as well as making notes of what was said. A note-taker should be employed for this, either a volunteer or perhaps the second in department if you have one. In very small departments you will have to use your judgement and discretion over who takes the notes.

Guideline 3   Invite only those who need to be at the meeting to attend

Too many people are often invited to meetings who, while they need to be informed, do not actually need to be in attendance. Think carefully about who should attend and who should be informed. By making your circulation list wider than your invitation list, you can cut down on unnecessary attendees. Make this known to others if you feel you are attending meetings when there really is no need!

Guideline 4   End the meeting on time

Always try to end the meeting on time, but try not to cut off important and essential discussion. The two things that really irritate people about meetings are those that go on well beyond the published end time and those where the chair of the meeting cuts off important discussion and guillotines debate that is felt by the staff to be important. If necessary, ask staff to agree an extension to the meeting in order to complete the debate, and set a time limit.

Guideline 5   Follow up the meeting with minutes ASAP

A meeting is reinforced by the minutes. Attached to those minutes there could be an action plan where the outcomes of the meeting are restated and those responsible for taking on board a task or commitment are identified. This will act as a reminder to those who agree to do something but will also mean that meetings are perceived as effective by those who attended. If an issue is brought up that involves another department or section of the school, then communicate just that segment of the minutes to the other party. They will not need to see the whole meeting agenda and minutes, but may be interested in the discussion that included their subject area or area of responsibility.

MEETINGS AS MOANING SESSIONS

Too often meetings in departments are dominated by staff who see it as an opportunity to offload their stress, frustration and grievances. In this situation the meeting turns into a moaning session and people leave feeling worse than they did at the start of the meeting. More often than not, there is a character in the meeting who can be described as the departmental cynic; no matter what suggestions are put forward, he or she meets it with a wholly negative attitude. There may also be a dominant member of staff with a personal agenda who will disrupt the meeting. Both of these situations can be effectively dealt with:

❏ Domination of a discussion by one person
  – Use direct questions to others.
  – Avoid looking at the dominant person when asking questions.
  – Privately chat to the dominant person and indicate that his or her dominance is disrupting the meeting by effectively disenfranchising others in the department.
❏ Argumentative people
  – Revert to questions from an open forum.
  – Be direct and point out the time wasting.
❏ Separate discussions in meetings
  – Overlook them if they are not intrusive.
  – If they are dominating, invite open discussion of the issue they are debating.
  – Remain silent until the group 'twigs'.
❏ Timid people in meetings
  – Know their areas of expertise and ask direct questions.
  – Involve them in meeting preparation.
❏ Antagonistic group members
  – Clarify the purpose of the meeting.
  – Offer a free expression period.
  – Try to discover their deep-rooted problems on a one-to-one basis.
❏ People who always answer questions with questions
  – Redirect it to the group or back at the individual.

It seems that up and down the country every department has a departmental cynic. They are the ones who have been there many years, seen it, done it, tried it out before (whatever the new initiative is), know that it won't work and therefore won't even bother trying to comply with your wishes. They've read the book, seen the film, bought the T-shirt! Dealing with these people is an art. One effective way is to prime them carefully before a meeting. If you know that a new initiative is going to be met with a long loud sigh and an attack by the departmental cynic, invite the cynic to meet with you before the meeting and appraise him or her of what is going to come up. Words to the following effect have proved useful and effective. *'Thank you for coming to see me (Name). Now, as you know, we are going to discuss X at the next meeting and I would really value your input on this subject. I know that you have strong views (or had experience of something similar). When this agenda item comes up I would like you to apprise the department of the problems, pitfalls and issues so that we can then concentrate on how we can avoid them in the future.'* This approach allows cynics to have a platform for their views, but avoids the drip attack so common in meetings, where they lie in wait and ambush you at strategic points, usually with the phrase *'And another thing. . .'* It also allows you to set the tone of the meeting as a positive one, thus: *'To start our next agenda item, I've asked (Name) to talk us through the problems, issues and pitfalls. This will help us to address the problems and come to a decision about how we can best implement the change without falling into the traps.'* It would, of course, be wise to set a time limit for the cynic's talk or invite the cynic to table a paper on the issues to avoid him or her dominating the meeting.

You cannot underestimate the help of a colleague in making meetings effective. In large departments where there is a person who is named as deputy head of department or second in charge (2iC), it is always a useful ploy to agree strategy with them before meetings. Conflict will nearly always occur when meetings take place. Sometimes the conflict is not easy to detect. It can arise simply from people being non-participants in the meeting. Sitting quietly, saying nothing, but as soon as the meeting finishes they become very vocal about the issues raised in the meeting. More often than not the conflict arises when people see a change in their working conditions that is detrimental or new to them. If you know that an agenda item will invoke a two-party response, ie one faction in favour and the other not in favour, you must allow some of that conflict to manifest itself by healthy debate. It is here that the 2iC will come in useful. Before the meeting, agree that the debate will be allowed to proceed but agree a cut-off time. The 2iC can then interrupt the debate and require that you, the head of department, make a decision. If the 2iC also points out that you are the one paid to make decisions, then you can interject and, on the balance of the debate, make a decision. This ploy will allow for debate, but allow you to take a decision without appearing to cut off the debate. Developing a close working relationship with your 2iC is vital to good departmental management.

Conflict will most often arise in meetings, but it is not the only place where it can manifest itself. The following principles apply while managing conflict either in meetings or at other times.

Ways to stop a conflict from escalating

1. Think about your own needs and those of your colleague. What outcome are you looking for and what is it that your colleague would like you to do? If possible, find this out before you begin to tackle the issue.
2. Do not let the situation inflame or escalate. If tempers are becoming frayed, take time out and suggest that another meeting be convened to discuss the problem. Make it clear that if there is a problem it will not simply go away and that it must be addressed at some time. Calling off the initial meeting is not a sign of your defeat or their success.
3. Do not use power or authority as a first step. Use it as a final resort. Demanding that someone follow your 'instructions' will only build up resentment. Influence is the best way to achieve conflict resolution.
4. Try to ensure that you let the other person know that you are aware of their needs and that if at all possible you will meet them. Point out that you may not be able to meet all of their needs but you will try to meet as many as possible without compromising your position and those of your colleagues.
5. When proposing a solution, propose it from the viewpoint of the other party. Point out which of their needs are being met and, if something cannot be met, explain why this cannot be met.

Points to consider when offering solutions

1. Picture how each party will benefit from the proposed solution. If you have a solution in mind, think about how it will affect each and every party. Make sure that when you talk through the solution, you address the needs of others before the needs of yourself and the school. People are naturally more inclined to think of their own welfare than the welfare of others. Remember that everyone needs to be heard before they will listen, so how you present the solution is as important as the solution itself.
   ❏ Present without contempt for the other parties (this includes the SMT).
   ❏ Do not present with anger.

❏ Do not be authoritarian.
❏ Do not be defeatist.

2. Don't talk before you are prepared to reach an agreement. Make sure that you have negotiated to the end of the line before you present a solution.

3. Demonstrate goodwill. Make it clear that solutions offered and accepted, even if they are the result of compromise, will not affect either party in the continuation of good working relationships. If the other party feels that you will bear a grudge because you had in some way to compromise, then more conflict may result, not less!

4. Make important points in the middle. Don't begin your presentation with the most important points and don't end with the most important points. Set the scene, then present the solution point by point, ending with a summary of the benefits to all parties of the solution offered.

5. If conflict cannot be resolved ask for help. If a situation is getting to the point where there can be no useful dialogue, you must ask for help. Try to involve another mutually acceptable colleague. A fear of staff is that conflict can end up with the SMT, thereby damaging one or the other party's credibility. Try to involve another colleague, eg the head of another department, to act as an independent mediator.

6. Be as flexible as you can. Often conflict results from the perception that there is no flexibility. Try not to dominate and talk all the time, as this often appears to be defensive. If you feel that you are dominating, ask for suggestions from the other party as to how they would proceed. Flexibility means taking on board ideas, it does not mean capitulating to every request.

7. Try not to disagree or dismiss ideas immediately. Even if you know that a suggestion from the other party is not feasible, immediate dismissal or disagreement often hardens the other's resolve. Consider their suggestions and provide at a later time reasoned argument against the suggestion or idea, and it is more likely to be accepted.

8

THE ROLE OF THE MENTOR

*'How dreadful knowledge of the truth can be when
there's no help in the truth.'*
Sophocles, Oedipus Rex

Traditionally mentors have been seen as necessary for certain categories of teachers only, such as newly qualified teachers, trainee teachers and failing teachers. The notion of a mentor for sound, effective, experienced staff is still a relatively new one. There is role for the head of department or subject leader to be a mentor to all staff that teach within his or her department or subject area. This will mean taking on board a role that is substantially different from that outlined in Chapter 9 (performance management), though the basics of being an effective mentor apply in both cases.

This chapter will look at the role of the mentor, how to establish productive mentoring relationships and how a mentor can effectively deal with the wide variety of staff that he or she will be responsible for, in particular:

❑ trainee teachers;
❑ NQTs;
❑ newly appointed staff;
❑ part-time staff;
❑ experienced staff;
❑ failing staff;
❑ non-teaching staff.

Taking on the role of a mentor often comes as a tied-in package with the responsibility of being part of the management structure of the school. Fletcher (2000) provides a handy summary of what mentoring is. She states that mentoring is:

❑ active education of the mentee;
❑ concerned with personal and professional development of the mentee;

❏   about easing transitions and ensuring development;
❏   responsive to individual strengths, values and needs of the mentor and mentee;
❏   about compassion and an acknowledgement that mistakes are inevitable;
❏   recognizing which mistakes are acceptable and which are not.

We must also recognize that being a mentor is also about learning as well as imparting one's own knowledge and experience. All of the above also apply to the mentor as well as the mentee.

THE NATURE OF MENTOR/MENTEE RELATIONSHIPS

Like any other human relationship, a mentoring relationship depends on an understanding of the values and expectations that both parties will have for each other and for the job they are engaged in. There is a need to develop empathy for the other person's feelings and needs. Where the relationship differs is in its professional nature. A mentor must convey the standards, norms, values and vision of the school to the mentees and offer support and challenges to the mentees as they carry out their day-to-day tasks. In order to develop a healthy mentoring relationship, a progressive development needs to take place. This development will in part necessitate the imparting of knowledge, skills, and understanding of the values of the school, with a resultant increase in competence of those being mentored.

Stages in mentoring relationship development

Mentoring relationships develop in a number of stages (see Figure 8.1).

Stage 1   Introduction

This stage is a crucial one if the person allocated to the mentor is a new appointee, an NQT or a trainee teacher. The mentor and mentee need to become acquainted. It is during this stage that the scene is set with respect to common interests, shared goals, values, professional goals etc. This stage should not be rushed; it does take time for the mentor and mentee to become acquainted with one another's goals and interests.

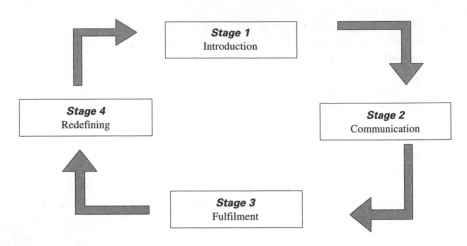

Figure 8.1 *The stages of mentor relationships*

Stage 2   Communication

This stage will see the mentor and mentee agree the procedures for the mentoring process. It is worthwhile pointing out here that the procedures may already be set out by the governing body of the school and this stage is about the mentor clearly explaining the procedures and, where possible, altering procedures to encompass the input of the mentee. It is vital that both parties are clear about the role that the mentor has and that the role is clarified as a non-judgemental one, as opposed to the role of, say, an appraiser or the person responsible for performance management. The needs and expectations of both parties need to be made explicit. Any problems with the mentoring process should become apparent at this stage, before the actual mentoring process begins.

Stage 3   Fulfilment

This is the active stage of the mentoring process. The agreed procedure is put into practice and the process of observation, feedback, and target setting is implemented. This stage may have a variable time-scale and may last for weeks, months or, in extreme cases, years. For most effective mentoring, however, the time-scale needs to be appropriate to the challenges and tasks set.

Stage 4   Redefining

When the person or persons working with the mentor feel that their needs are met or when tasks, challenges and expectations are met, the mentoring process is in effect at an end and a period of redefinition of the tasks, needs, challenges and expectations is needed.

All of the above stages are crucial to the fulfilment of positive mentoring experiences. Since this is the case, both the mentor and the mentee must clearly communicate expectations. It is a failure to do this that, in many cases, leads to a breakdown in the mentoring process and the mentoring relationship. During stages 1 and 2, a number of expectations will be aired and must be agreed upon. Table 8.1 includes examples of the sorts of expectations that often arise at these stages.

Table 8.1 *Sample expectations from the first two stages of the mentoring process*

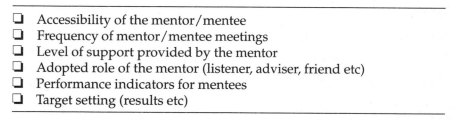

❑   Accessibility of the mentor/mentee
❑   Frequency of mentor/mentee meetings
❑   Level of support provided by the mentor
❑   Adopted role of the mentor (listener, adviser, friend etc)
❑   Performance indicators for mentees
❑   Target setting (results etc)

These early stages are all about getting to know each other. In some commercial situations the choice of mentor may be up to the individual employee. Should this be the case, it is common for employees to 'sound out' a few mentors and seek to establish a relationship with one that meets their expectations. In schools this is often not possible. The nature of teaching is such that mentors are often drawn from within a subject area. If your subject area is small, say a humanities subject, then there may only be a head of department and one other full-time teacher. In this case the choice is limited. Some schools, in recognition of this, do allow a more or less free choice of mentor and the line manager acts only in the capacity of appraiser. Should a free or limited choice of mentor be available to staff then there are several important factors that staff will evaluate in order to initiate the relationship:

❑ personality similarities;
❑ management similarities;
❑ levels of support on offer;
❑ degree of personal connectivity (eg age, background, education);
❑ ability to offer subject support.

What leads a person to link with a specific mentor, given a free choice, is a complex matter. How two people link and work together when the choice is not a free one requires a greater degree of planning and training by the management of the school to have any chance of success. When choice is not an option, we rely on the notion of professionalism in order to overcome these difficulties. Being professional should mean that you are able to see beyond some of those factors that people place emphasis on in order to initiate a good working relationship, ie personality and personal connectivity.

THE NATURE OF MENTORING

An initial response to the question 'What is mentoring?' usually brings responses that include the notion of experts sharing knowledge and understanding. This is understandable as the image of the mentor usually focuses on the expertise that the mentor has as being one of the reasons that the person was chosen for the role in the first place. In teaching, this expertise is usually related not to the specific subject knowledge that can be imparted to the mentee, or for that matter the pupils, but the pedagogic knowledge that the mentor has built up over many years of teaching. In one relationship, say that between the mentor and an NQT or trainee teacher, the initial response of the mentor to the question may well be about imparting some of that pedagogic knowledge to enable the trainee or NQT to develop as a teacher. The trainee or NQT, however, may also wish to tap into the mentor's actual subject knowledge. They will recognize that knowing a fact or concept for themselves is not the same as being able to teach that same fact or concept to their pupils. The expectations here then may result in conflict. The mentor's expectations are that the trainee or NQT will require pedagogical input; the trainee or NQT, however, may need input related to the content and the level at which that content has to be taught. As an experienced teacher, the mentor will understand how pupils gain subject knowledge in their subject and, therefore, how that knowledge has to be repackaged in order to be effective. They will in turn have the experience to know that different teaching styles may be required in order to achieve the lesson outcomes. But how can this be achieved if the mentor's subject knowledge differs from that of the mentee? The answer must lie in the process that has been set up by the management of the school to provide the links between the appropriate mentor and the mentee. It is easy to see, therefore, that the choice of mentor can be crucial to the success of the process. It is also now self-evident that the initial stages of the mentoring process must set out what the mentor is able to offer the mentee in terms of support and help.

The role of the mentor as one of sharing expertise is central to the relationship, therefore it is wise to have a plan for how such expertise may be identified and shared. The following few suggestions describe an example of shared expectations and experiences for the mentoring process in planning for teaching, and would help to define common ground for the person you have to be a mentor for:

❑ Define the times when mentoring sessions will take place (if not already dictated by the management of mentoring within the school).
❑ Discuss and agree goals for the coming
  – term;
  – year.
❑ Agree performance indicators for the goals so that you both know when the goals have been achieved.
❑ Gain consensus for the accepted lesson planning process within the department (ie the level and amount of detail expected in planning and the right of access to plans by you and other line managers).
❑ Describe your own procedures for long-, medium- and short-term planning.
❑ Induct the mentee into the various planning aids/tools that exist (either paper based or utilizing ICT).
❑ Agree a programme of review and evaluation of lesson plans.

COMMUNICATION IN MENTORING

The success of any mentoring relationship will in part come down to the effectiveness of the communication between the various parties involved. The communication skills outlined in Chapter 6 will be invaluable here. One of the big mistakes in communication is not setting the context in which the communication will take place. The context will decide what expectations the mentor and mentee have of the purpose of the communication. For a newly qualified teacher, having their lessons observed and then being given feedback on the lesson is a normal state. The NQT will have been observed on many occasions and will have had their fair share of positive and negative feedback. An experienced teacher, however, may not be as used to detailed feedback. Even the level of lesson planning expected from an NQT and an experienced teacher will vary. Setting the context of the observation is therefore vital for ensuring that there is constructive feedback and a positive mentoring session. Before any mentoring session takes place, a planning session is needed where the context of the session is explained. In the case of a lesson observation the following points need to be addressed:

❏ Is the lesson to be observed in full or in part?
❏ What aspects of the teaching and learning are being observed?
❏ What information is necessary before the observation can commence?
❏ What information is necessary before the mentoring session can commence?
❏ What performance indicators are being set for the lesson?

The process of mentoring will most likely revolve around the observations of a teacher's lessons and the feedback given to staff on those lessons. Observing lessons is a three-stage process:

1. Pre-observation meeting – where the parameters of the observation are discussed and agreed.
2. The observation itself – this may be a full lesson or part of a lesson or even a small sequence of lesson parts (eg starts, finishes etc).
3. The post-observation feedback – relating mainly to the parameters agreed beforehand.

Effective communication at all three stages is a must.

Not all mentoring will contain elements of school-based observation. Mentoring can take place in a variety of contexts and in a variety of ways. It may be a session that explores the professional development of the teacher in question and it may look at which aspects of continuing professional development are required to enable the mentee to realize his or her professional goals. Sometimes the mentoring session will consider aspects of the mentee's personal life, especially when these interact with the professional work of the mentee. This is probably the most difficult aspect of being a mentor. You must know your limitations and what you can effectively help with and what you cannot. In many cases, when a member of staff presents you with personal issues, either as their mentor or head of department, the most important thing to do is listen. It is vital that the person feels that they are listened to. The second most important thing is to be non-judgemental. Whatever your personal view of the problem, they have not come to you for a judgement; they have probably come for a friendly ear to listen to their problems. Once you are aware of the situation, you must then weigh up what advice you can give, if any.

MENTORING UNDER-PERFORMANCE IN STAFF

At some stage in your career you will come up against the issue of mentoring under-performance. This is a very delicate situation that needs very careful and professional handling. Under-performance is a challenge in any situation, but where it involves close working colleagues who may directly or indirectly be affected by that member of staff it can be more challenging. Chris Woodhead, the former chief inspector of schools, made a very damaging statement regarding the existence of 15,000 under-performing teachers in 1995. The media explosion, almost calling for heads to roll in schools up and down the land, was difficult to handle. But whatever the figure, 15,000 or 15, even one under-performing teacher in a school can be very damaging. There is a responsibility on both the mentor and the teacher identified as under-performing to take firm action to bring performance back up to speed. Ofsted's 1995 annual report stated that *'Inspection… shows that the performance of a small minority of teachers is consistently weak'*. It was this small minority that Chris Woodhead identified as 15,000 teachers, approximately 4 per cent of the teaching force. The report went on to state that *'it is rare for steps to be taken to resolve the problems they cause'*. The person in the front line who may be delegated the job of resolving the problems is likely to be the head of department. Clearly the problem needs to be identified. That may happen as a result of the performance management process or the inspection process. It may also result from parental complaint. It is most likely that the problems may lie in one or more of the following categories:

❏   subject knowledge;
❏   pupil expectation (usually too low, sometimes too high);
❏   discipline;
❏   marking;
❏   adherence to school policy;
❏   time management;
❏   planning (short, medium, long term).

It is important to note that heads of department are not the people responsible for initiating disciplinary procedures. The head of department will, however, be involved closely should such proceedings be initiated by the senior management team. In the role of a mentor you have a difficult path to tread. You need to be supportive of staff, seen as non-judgemental, fair and willing to help the under-performing member of staff to improve. Once any action is initiated by senior management, you need to make sure that you understand the implications of your role and that the member of staff is also aware of your role. Once an agreed procedure is in place (agreed by the teacher and the senior management team), it must be adhered to.

Mentoring staff in this situation means that you have to recognize the stance that the member of staff may take in response to your efforts to 'help'. This will range from silence to hostile responses. Table 8.2 outlines various stances that under-performing staff may take. Experience shows that people will inevitably display more than one stance. You, as the mentor, will have to be prepared to deal with all of the stances the member of staff may adopt.

Table 8.2 *Typical stances taken by under-performing staff and suggested responses (adapted from Bush and Middlewood, 1997)*

Hostile/Aggressive	Deal calmly with aggression, do not respond aggressively, be assertive
Complainer	Listen, acknowledge the complaint but do not accept it as a sole cause of under-performance
Silent/Unresponsive	Gently probe with simple questions, listen and pause at the end of each question as if a response were expected
Over-agreeable	Check that any response is realistic. Try to get the person to be open and honest
Negativist	Be positive, find instances where praise can genuinely be given. Present the upbeat side of problems and their associated solutions
Know-it-alls	Ensure that you have hard evidence. It may be necessary to 'agree to disagree'
Indecisives	Provide incentives/benefits to taking the suggested approach to solving the problem. Have 'hard' and fixed deadlines

NON-TEACHING STAFF

Some areas employ technical help or have the regular assistance of learning support staff. Before any mentoring takes place, the head of department must be clear about who has responsibility for that member of staff. It is important to note that all staff that fall under your remit need to be included in the mentoring process. A sure-fire way of creating a division between staff (teaching and non-teaching) is to practise selective mentoring of the teaching staff only. In the same way that teachers deserve attention to their professional development, so too do the non-teaching staff. The process is similar, but obviously the procedures will differ and the focus of the mentoring and performance indicators will differ also.

The key to good mentoring is being prepared. The key to a good mentoring session is effective two-way communication.

9

MANAGING STAFF PERFORMANCE

'A teacher who does not equip his pupils with the rudimentary tools to discover truth is substituting indoctrination for teaching.'
Professor Richard Peters

Performance management has been introduced and is seen by the DfES as a sign that the school has a commitment to the development of all teachers. One of its stated aims is to ensure job satisfaction for staff, along with high levels of expertise and progression of staff in their chosen profession (DfEE, 2000). They state that effective performance management 'helps teachers to meet the needs of children and raise standards' (DfEE, 2000, p 1). The guidance issued by the DfEE in 2000 is summarized here and forms the basis this chapter.

HOW CAN PERFORMANCE MANAGEMENT HELP?

Performance management is seen as a way of helping schools to improve. In the current climate of league tables and accountability for raising standards, this is a natural step. It sets out a framework for teachers, their managers and the management of the school as a whole, including governors, to in effect assess effective teaching and leadership. The primary concern is that of benefit to the pupils, the teachers and the schools themselves.

The DfES sees two major benefits to performance management: 1) benefits to the pupils of effective, focused teachers; 2) benefits to the teachers from an assessment of their needs and their continuing professional development.

There have been a number of criticisms of performance management, not least from the unions, who fear a return to the payment by results system that dominated Victorian education. Those fears have not been translated into practice, with the first round of performance management leading to many teachers applying for and getting acceptance of their bid to cross the pay threshold. Over 90 per cent of those teachers who applied were granted access to the post-threshold pay scale.

The notion of target setting, monitoring of teaching and evaluations of staff is not new in schools and many establishments have in place long-standing procedures for just this sort of performance management. It was therefore seen as the next step to introduce the best practice nationally.

That existing best practice was looked at and documented by the DfEE and a number of characteristics drawn up, exemplified by:

❑ a commitment to the attainment and welfare of pupils at their school;
❑ an appreciation of the crucial role that teachers play;
❑ an atmosphere of trust between teacher and team leader, which allows them to evaluate strengths and identify areas for development;
❑ encouragement to share good practice; and
❑ the integration of performance management with the overall approach to managing the school.

(DfEE, 2000)

Performance management is a team exercise. There is no one person in the school that can, or should, effectively assess the work of all teachers. While the headteacher may have the overall responsibility for the quality of teaching within the school, he or she cannot effectively assess all staff. It has therefore fallen to team leaders (heads of department in large schools or subject leaders) to assist in the performance management process.

A PHILOSOPHY FOR PERFORMANCE MANAGEMENT

If performance management is to work at all, it must become a part of the culture of the school, a culture that is subscribed to by all of the staff. There must be a sharing of the commitment to performance management and a support of the need for continuous improvement. In turn, there must also be recognition of the success of schools, teachers, ancillary staff and, most importantly, pupils.

In order for this to become a reality there needs to be a commitment to raising standards by all. There must be a culture that supports the continuing professional development of all staff and a system of performance management and recognition within the school that is manageable and not cumbersome. It is also necessary for that system to be open, fair and not simply a bolt-on to the day-to-day running and management of the school.

Schools must produce a policy for performance management and, more importantly, a procedure to see that that policy is implemented. The policy must be a fair one that allows for all teachers to be treated on an equal basis and that is simple to put into practice. As a policy describes best practice, the procedure that implements the policy should allow for the sharing of that good practice between teachers. Performance management is not a one-off process that assesses performance once. It is part of a cycle and, as such, the performance management cycle must be clearly understood by you, the head of department or subject leader, and by the staff over whom you have direct or indirect control. In the case of staff who teach in more than one subject area, the management of the school will advise heads of department and subject leaders of their input to the performance management profile of the member of staff concerned.

THE PERFORMANCE MANAGEMENT CYCLE

There are three stages to the performance management cycle (see Figure 9.1).

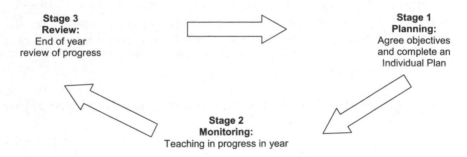

Figure 9.1 *The performance management cycle (after DfEE, 2000)*

Planning

The head of department or subject leader (in some cases this will be the team leader) should discuss and record priorities and objectives with each of the teachers in their team. They must discuss how progress will be monitored and what instruments for monitoring will be used (eg observation forms, statistics on pupil results etc.).

Each teacher and team leader should agree at the start of the review cycle what should be the focus of the teacher's work during the year. It is important, therefore, for new heads of department or subject leaders to get to know the staff and their role within the school and in particular within the department. At the outset, there should be a discussion based on a clear job description; eg 'Teacher of English, accountable to the head of department, teaching English to Key Stage 3, 4 and at post 16'.

The next step is to discuss the individual teacher's work-related priorities, the needs of the pupils for whom the teacher is responsible and their personal priorities. Once these are clear, the next step is to agree specific objectives for the coming year or performance management cycle. The prime focus of this discussion should be the progress of pupils, and the way the teacher can best engage and stretch pupils through his or her teaching.

It is important to note that agreeing objectives does not mean itemizing every activity. Objectives will need to cover pupil progress as well as ways of developing and improving teachers' professional practice.

The objectives set for any individual teacher must be clear and concise. They need to be challenging but not unrealistic. They should also be flexible, as they may need amending or replacing during the performance management period.

There is no hard and fast rule about how many objectives should be agreed by a teacher. The first round of performance management reviews suggests that four objectives would be the norm for the vast majority of staff.

The team leader has a specific role and he or she must:

❑ ensure that each teacher understands the set objectives and their implications;
❑ understand where factors outside a teacher's control might affect the attainment of any objective or set of objectives;
❑ ensure that discussions with the teacher take place at the start of the cycle;
❑ ensure that the objectives relate to the objectives in the school development plan.

A teacher's Individual Plan records that teacher's responsibilities and objectives.

Monitoring

The teacher who is the subject of the review and the team leader will need to keep progress over the specified period under review. If it is felt by one or the other that support for the teacher is needed, then arrangements for this must be put into place.

It is essential that attention to progress of individual teachers be given during the year. This has time implications for busy heads of department or subject leaders. There are also implications for staff development, with a clear implication that there will be a commitment to staff development. There may already be methods to monitor progress, such as short informal discussions and classroom observation. The teacher and the team leader will need to discuss any supportive action that may be needed and ensure that the development page of the teacher's Individual Plan is kept up to date.

Classroom observation is seen as accepted good practice. The days of closing the classroom door to all but the pupils and their teacher are long gone. Whatever approach is used, classroom observation should be set out clearly. Many schools find it useful to use a standard pro-forma. In planning any observation, it is important to bear in mind the following:

❑ Observation requires preparation and training of the observer.
❑ There must be a clear understanding on the part of the teacher and the team leader of why the observation is happening.
❑ It needs to be structured, with agreed areas of observation.
❑ Full, constructive feedback takes place as soon as is practicable.

Review

The teacher and the team leader should meet to review any achievements over the year and evaluate the teacher's overall performance, taking account of progress against objectives.

The cycle is designed to take place over a normal school year and will be linked to the school's overall planning for management and target setting.

A performance review is an opportunity for the teacher and team leader to reflect on the teacher's overall performance in a structured way. It should be designed to recognize any achievements and discuss areas for improvement and professional development. The focus of the review should be on how to raise performance and improve effectiveness. It should involve:

- ❏ a review of the teacher's essential day-to-day tasks;
- ❏ a recognition of the teacher's strengths and achievements;
- ❏ a confirmation of the action agreed with the teacher during informal discussions;
- ❏ an identification of any areas for development and how these will be met;
- ❏ a recognition of any personal development needs.

The team leader must make a professional judgement about the overall effectiveness of the teacher. As head of department or subject leader, you will have to do this and you must, therefore, take account of the stage the teacher is at in his or her career, eg an NQT or advanced skills teacher.

If a teacher is unhappy with any aspect of the review, then his or her concerns can be raised with the headteacher. Where the headteacher is the team leader, the teacher can raise the issue with the Chair of Governors.

The outcomes of performance review will be used to inform pay decisions, for example for awarding double performance increments for outstanding performance up to the performance threshold, and for awarding discretionary performance pay points above the threshold, for Advanced Skills Teachers and teachers in the leadership group. Information from performance reviews will provide evidence for assessment at the performance threshold.

SETTING OBJECTIVES

Any objectives set for teachers will usually arise from discussion between team leaders and individual teachers about the department's priorities for the coming year. This may typically involve targeting the progress of a group of pupils that is not meeting expectations or the identification of a small number of named pupils. It might be a priority for the department to implement new procedures arising from new policies or develop approaches or classroom-based teaching techniques that will help pupil progress, eg better classroom management skills, the introduction of a new scheme or the inclusion of a literacy/numeracy strategy.

Objectives set by team leaders are expected to cover pupil progress and professional development for the teacher in question. If you work within a large department then it may be appropriate to set management/leadership objectives for teachers with responsibilities.

Objectives about pupil progress should be based on what is already known about the pupils, ie a baseline of robust evidence. The school has access to a number of sources, such as external and internal assessments, PANDAs and benchmarking data, to set targets in the school's development plan. Heads of department and subject leaders will want to refer to these data and then discuss with individual teachers how their particular contribution should be focused and formulate the teacher's objective accordingly.

Professional development objectives may include observation of other teachers (both from within the school or at other schools, eg Beacon status schools), mentoring, good practice development and training. The career aspirations of the teacher will help in setting these objectives.

The scope of objectives must be appropriate to teachers' job responsibilities, hence the need to have secure and robust job descriptions that accurately reflect the work of the teacher in question. Headteachers will have objectives for pupil progress at school level, while as a head of subject you may wish to look at progress by year group. Teachers within departments will focus on work with individual cohorts, groups or individuals. They should also be appropriate to teachers' circumstances, eg part-time working or disability. Teachers and team leaders will want to discuss how the objectives should be achieved and ensure that professional development needs are considered in school planning. Resource implications will need to be taken into account, such as supply cover or costs associated with development activities.

It is good practice for objectives to be *clear and precise* to allow progress to be measured. The exact form will vary: what is important is that the planning discussions are based on an understanding of pupils' prior attainment, that teacher and team leader agree how they will measure progress and that annual reviews involve an assessment of progress actually achieved in the circumstances.

Teachers should never be discouraged from setting challenging objectives, even if, at the end of the performance management cycle, these objectives are not achieved in full. The reasons for this can be many and varied, including a range of reasons that lie beyond an individual teacher's control. Meeting challenging objectives will be a good way for teachers to show their substantial and sustained performance and help develop their careers. When assessing overall performance, heads of department and subject leaders must consider how challenging the objectives that were set have been. A teacher who has not quite achieved challenging objectives may have contributed as much as, or more than, a teacher who has met less challenging objectives in full.

Objectives must always relate to the situation that exists in your school and the pupils in the teacher's classes. Headteachers and team leaders will need to decide how individual objectives relate to school-level planning.

ROLES AND RESPONSIBILITIES

The head has overall responsibility for implementing the school's perform-ance management policy and ensuring that the performance management reviews actually take place. The head must also:

❑ ensure that other team leaders within the school carry out their responsibilities;
❑ ensure that any Individual Plans and standards are agreed for all teachers;
❑ ensure that the monitoring of teaching takes place and that feedback given allows the teacher both to reflect on his or her performance and to participate fully in the discussion.

The governing body has a strategic role to perform. The context for the performance management policy is to be set by the school's development plan. The governing body must agree this. They are also responsible for agreeing the school's performance management policy and for ensuring that the performance of teachers at the school is regularly reviewed.

MANAGING WEAK PERFORMANCE

Good management, with clear expectations and appropriate support, will go a long way towards identifying and handling any weaknesses in performance.

The performance review does not form a part of any disciplinary or dismissal procedures that may be taken by the school management against an individual teacher. However, where information from the review gives cause for concern about any teacher's performance in the execution of their duties, it may lead to a decision by the management of the school and/or the governors to investigate and record performance more intensively.

10

STAFF SELECTION AND INTERVIEWING

*'I don't want any yes-men around me. I want everybody to
tell me the truth even if it costs them their job.'*
Samuel Goldwyn

If staff is the key to a successful school then the interview and selection
procedure must be robust and provide the best candidate for the job on
offer.

Many schools advertise for new staff but few are really prepared to follow
a professional selection and interview process that seeks to attract and filter
out the best candidates. Many schools are still reliant on the old, standard
methods of a *TES* advert, a short tour of the school, perhaps a brief teaching
session and a panel interview. But does this method necessarily produce
the best candidate?

A number of common selection and interview mistakes that are often
made where a school does not have a standard policy and procedure for
interviewing new teachers are listed below. Avoid as many of these as you
can, all of them if possible, when looking to appoint new staff, whether
they are NQTs or experienced staff.

Procrastination

A failure to begin the search process early is the source of many hiring
mistakes. Often the structure of the school year and the traditional 'resignation dates' are the source of this. Although it is not possible to alter the
resignation dates, for very good reasons, one way to avoid the last-minute
panic is to set up a bank of job specifications (not job descriptions) for each
department. The head of department, in consultation with the senior
management team, must be the lead force here. With any change in middle
management there may be a need to look carefully at the specifications to
ensure that they still fit with the philosophy of the new subject or pastoral
leader. In industry the average search for new staff takes 90–120 days.

The halo effect

At some point you will interview the outstanding candidate, impeccably dressed, well spoken, dynamic, visionary, alert and a whole host of other adjectives that make the perfect employee. Psychological studies have shown that a number of other positive attributes are assumed to be associated with this person, such as intelligence, humour, competence etc. It is important not to be taken in by the sharp suit and the good looks. As an interviewing panel, probing questions need to be asked (however, this is true for all candidates) and answers analysed carefully.

Employing the best, even if they don't fit!

Too often, interview panels will seek only to employ the best, most highly qualified candidate that they can, without thinking about whether the highest qualification is necessarily the best for the job to be done. Faced with two candidates, one with a third-class honours degree and average A levels and one with straight As and a PhD, which would you choose? Academic prowess is not the only quality a teacher should have; in fact other qualities may be of more importance in your school, such as the ability to relate to low achievers. Sometimes those with a PhD cannot understand why pupils find difficulty with what to them is a relatively simple concept, whereas the third-class honours student knows the struggle the pupil has to go through in order to understand.

Matching the candidate's capabilities with the job in hand is important. The last thing both they and you would want is a bored teacher.

Asking leading questions

The art of questioning, as teachers know, is a complex one that requires skill and forethought. Ask any examiner and they will say that the most difficult part of an exam is setting the questions. All too often, leading questions are asked in interviews that allow quick candidates to provide the required answer, regardless of their real views or opinions on the issue, eg 'We have a strong uniform policy in the school set out by the governors. What is your view on school uniforms?' The reply will hardly be, 'I don't believe in them', or 'Too much time is taken up with silly rules on uniforms.' The sharp candidate will give the required answer of support for the uniform. What then happens once they are in post may be a different matter.

Talking too much

Saying too much is a common mistake. An effective interviewer listens for 80 per cent of the time. Unfortunately, human nature often means that during the interview the members of the panel use this as an opportunity to sell the school and say how wonderful it is. All of this should have been done before, so that those who turn up on the day will already want to come to the school and are there to sell themselves to you. The interview process is a long one. As a rule of thumb, a panel interview for an NQT should take no more than 45 minutes and for a middle manager 90 minutes (this excludes any tours or exercises, eg teaching a class).

Blank sheets

Amazingly, many people sit through an interview and make no notes at all. How are you going to compare the candidates if there has been no note taking in answer to specific questions?

Accepting generalizations

As candidates know they have to sell themselves in interviews, should you accept what they say at face value? For example: 'My A-level pass rate was 100 per cent for the last three years.' Yes, but how many candidates were entered? If specific claims are made, what and where is the evidence to back this up?

Ill-advised questions

Some interview panels are still ignorant of employment law and stray into areas where they should not, eg marital status, sexual orientation, family plans, husband or wife's status, religion (with the exception of denominational schools) etc. Asking inappropriate questions may lead to claims under the Equal Opportunities Act if candidates feel they were disadvantaged during the interview.

Indifference

As an employer, the governors are duty bound to take reasonable care when checking a candidate's references or qualifications. It may be exhaustive and difficult to check every detail, but you must make sure that the major details are correct, on the basis that the minor ones will most probably be correct if the major ones are. Is that person really an Oxford graduate? Do they really hold a PhD from Harvard? Should these turn out to be correct, then in all probability they really do belong to the Tufty Club and collect stamps as a hobby.

The counter offer

This is most likely to happen when NQTs are being considered. At the start of their spring experience, many NQTs will make multiple applications to schools for jobs. Sadly this is another effect of the system we have in place. In some countries, eg France, jobs are allocated, not applied for, and in others, eg Ethiopia, the allocation could be at the other end of the country from where the student resides. Here we battle in the marketplace for good quality candidates. If the preparation work is done and the attitude of the school is right, from the very first contact with the candidates to the way in which they are handled on the day of the interview, there is less chance of the candidate taking up the other offers that may be out there somewhere. The interview handcuff of offering the job to the candidate on the day and requiring a commitment is well established in schools. Many mature entrants to teaching find this an extraordinary state of affairs and an unfair burden to place on people who have to think carefully about their own situation and make major decisions that may involve moving to a new area with all the problems that brings. With the current shortage of teachers, especially in some subject areas such as maths and science, it is not now unusual for the candidate to interview the school. This has meant that some candidates will now defer their decision to take up a job offer in the knowledge that there are a number of jobs out there.

A MODEL SELECTION AND INTERVIEW PROCEDURE

Different schools will use different procedures to conduct interviews and select the best person for the job on offer. The following model is based on experience and does lead to an informed choice when short-listing candidates; it also provides a robust procedure should a candidate decide to challenge the decision of the panel on their eventual appointment.

The appointment procedure

Details of the post

Appointing new staff means that a reassessment of the balance of skills in the department can be made. Details of the post to be offered should be discussed with the senior management team and a written person specification and job description produced.

The person profile/specification

The work of the whole department should be considered and thought should be given to the type of person needed to fit in as a team member. It should be written to accomplish the objective of developing, enhancing and consolidating the work of the department.

The person specification should list as many of the qualities that you would want to see in the new member of staff as possible. They can be divided into the following categories:

❑ Education, training and qualifications
❑ Knowledge, skills and aptitudes
❑ Prior experiences
❑ Pedagogical approach

The exact details of what should be listed will depend on your requirements. Number the specifications so that a grid can be drawn up against which applications can be scrutinized.

Part of a person specification for a science post is reproduced below.

Job descriptions

The head is responsible for deploying and managing all staff. In many cases a job description will accompany any contract of employment. It is likely that the head of department will assist the head in drawing up such a job description. However, the existence of a job description does not mean that the employee cannot be called upon to carry out other duties. The head, governing body or proprietor of an independent school may ask – or instruct – an employee to carry out other duties provided:

❑ they are reasonable in relation to the employee's capabilities;
❑ they are necessary because of the particular circumstances; and

Person Specification for the Post of Science Teacher

PURPOSE

This person specification has been prepared for the fair screening and short-listing of applicants. It will form the basis of the interview and inform the decision-making process for the appointment of a full-time science teacher to the faculty of science.

The person specification is a picture of the knowledge, skills, aptitudes and experience that are necessary for effective and safe performance in the job advertised.

EDUCATION TRAINING AND QUALIFICATIONS

1. Qualified teacher under DfES regulations (or appropriate qualifications for appointment on a GTP programme)
2. Trained to teach all science to the end of KS3
3. Trained to teach Chemistry to KS4 and AS/A2
4. A second science subject to KS4
5. Good first degree in science
6. Higher degree in science/education (optional)
7. Good A levels in science or equivalent
8. Membership of professional institution(s)

KNOWLEDGE, SKILLS AND APTITUDES

1. An understanding of the requirements for science (NC 2000)
2. An awareness of the current regulations relating to the implementation of science in the national curriculum
3. An awareness of how pupils learn science
4. An appreciation of children's conceptual understanding in science
5. An ability to match teaching to learning
6. A knowledge of constructivism in teaching and learning
7. A knowledge of effective strategies for differentiation

❑ the employee is not being treated unfavourably compared to other similar employees.

Teachers should be consulted before job descriptions are finalized, but if agreement is not possible then the head may set out the responsibilities that a particular teacher is to undertake.

The advertisement

The governing body is required to advertise a vacancy 'in a manner likely in (its) opinion to bring it to the notice of persons (including employees) who are qualified to fill the post'.

Think carefully about the wording of an advertisement for the newspaper and don't forget local papers. If you look at the main destination for job adverts, the *TES*, many of the job adverts are indistinguishable from the rest. How will you make your job advert stand out from the crowd?

Information to candidates

Draw up a candidate package that includes details of the post, the school, its setting and the structure of the department. Include details of what is taught and how, with details of any schemes used and specifications taught. Add details about how the department is staffed (teaching and non-teaching) and the type of accommodation (eg would the teacher have their own base or be expected to travel from class to class?). Market your department and include any outside reference to the department's work from recent OFSTED reports or local inspections. Remember that you already work at the school and the idea is to market your school and department to attract the best candidates that you can. By providing full and frank information you will eliminate some potential applicants who would not, for example, be happy at teaching a certain scheme or moving bases etc.

Candidates should be given the following information:

❑ about the school;
❑ about the department;
❑ about the advertised post, eg the person specification and job description.

Candidates should also be informed if applications are to be made on a specified form or by letter and/or CV.

Candidate selection

Candidates whose applications appear to fit the person specification should be invited for interview. There is no limit to the number of persons who may be requested to come for interview, but the number invited must be agreed by the head of department and senior management, given the post that needs filling, the number of applicants and the time available for interview. By using a numbered grid and ticking those aspects of the person specification that candidates meet according to their applications and letters, you can produce an objective shortlist, which, if challenged, can easily be justified.

The interview

Before the interviews take place, decide on what will happen during the day, make arrangements for tours of the school, an opportunity to meet with the department and, if it is part of your procedure, a time to teach a specimen lesson. Remember that teaching the lesson will not be a full and true reflection of the candidates' ability as it will be taken out of context and will have limitations in that the candidates will not know the pupils. Do contact them well in advance to allow them to prepare for the lesson and give as much information as you can about what is expected of them.

Agree with the panel the questions to be asked and who is asking what question. It is important that you ask the same questions of each of the candidates, otherwise it will be difficult to make like-for-like comparisons. There is a need, therefore, to make arrangements for segregating the candidates before and after their individual interview.

Interview procedures should be agreed between all members of the panel prior to the start of the interviews. All candidates should be given equal opportunity to display their fitness for the post advertised. The entire panel should discuss each candidate before making a final decision. Candidates may be informed by letter or, more commonly, by word of mouth.

There are two Acts that have considerable bearing on the interview process, the Race Relations Act (1976) and the Sex Discrimination Act (1975). Nothing said or discussed, either in an interview or in the wording of an advertisement, must impute any suggestion of sex or race discrimination. With respect to the Rehabilitation of Offenders Act (1974), anyone employed in a school in a capacity involving contact with pupils under the age of 18 may not consider any convictions 'spent' and must declare them when applying for a job.

During the interview, any notes made by members of the panel to aid in selection must be kept in case an unsuccessful candidate challenges the decision of the panel. Be careful what you write about candidates during the interview, as they do have a legal right of access to your notes!

Should no candidates be felt suitable for appointment, then a re-advertisement may be necessary.

You are advised to check on any LEA/Employer guidelines as to what constitutes appropriate and/or inappropriate questions that may be asked during interview.

Appointment of NQTs

After 7 May 1999 all NQTs must satisfactorily complete an induction year (see circular 582/2001 for full details).

WAYS OF ASSESSING CANDIDATES

By far the commonest way of assessing ability for the job on offer is by an interview panel. Validity studies of panel interviews show that the resultant appointments have a value of between 0.15 and 0.20. This is a very low score, which implies that the panel interview is not accurate. Scores of above 0.5 would be needed to say with any confidence that the panel interview was a valid method of selection. But this is by no means the only way. There are a number of exercises that could be done in an effort to select the most appropriate candidate.

Group discussion

All the candidates are brought together as a committee or team and asked to discuss a number of items connected with the job, eg curriculum design, lesson development, pastoral issues. The members may be given roles to play and the interview panel will sit back, watch and take notes on how they perform.

In-tray

This is a common exercise for management jobs that is rarely extended to ordinary classroom teachers. Organizing and prioritizing are skills that all teachers need. The panel may devise some in-tray exercises that candidates must complete to show their level of organization and skill in dealing with a range of situations from handling parents to dealing with everyday items such as test results and score analysis

Role play (classroom teaching)

Many schools now ask candidates to teach in their subject specialism at short notice with no prior knowledge of the pupils. This can be valuable provided the right criteria are applied to those seeking to fulfil the role. This is often not a good test of some skills, eg classroom management.

Role play (management)

Another role play could be used in a group setting by allocating a management issue and asking candidates to show you how they would respond to that issue, eg interviewing a teacher who is under-performing.

Case study analysis

Again more often associated with management interviews, the case study approach will be designed to test decision-making skills in particular situations.

Psychometric testing

Some organizations use a form of psychometric testing as a part of their assessment process and selection procedure. The tests will fall into two broad categories

Ability and aptitude tests

These have been shown to be excellent indicators of future performance.

Measures of personality

The way that a person performs in their job is not solely due to their ability and aptitude. Their personality also plays an important part. These tests can provide a useful insight into an individual's style of behaviour and ways of interacting with other people.

AFTER THE INTERVIEW: PICKING UP THE PIECES

The interview debrief is one of the most difficult things for managers to conduct. After a day of intense, sometimes very stressful situations for candidates, you are then required to tell them where they went wrong and why they didn't get the job. It's a bit like kicking a person after they've fallen at the last hurdle. There are ways of conducting debrief sessions that will constructively help people improve on their technique at interviews. Rather than concentrate only on the negative aspects of an interview, it is most helpful to highlight good points and constructively criticize poor points.

The debrief

A positive start

Point out that, by making the final list, people will have already been successful in making most of the running. It is helpful here to say briefly what it was about their application that attracted you:

❑ a strong statement in support of an application;
❑ clearly set out information that is to the point;
❑ addressing the needs of the school as set out in the person specification;
❑ good presentation.

Letting the candidate know how they stood in the field is also a positive start, eg if there were 15 applications and only 3 called for interview, it means that 12 didn't even make the short-list (however, avoid this one if there was a very small field!).

Pre-interview work

Stress the importance of research before attending the interview. If it was shown during the interview that the candidate had conducted some research, then praise this. If it was clear that they had not, then impress upon them the need to know about a school before they come along. Also dispel any myths that the tour etc is not part of the interview process – it is.

Preparation for questions

Certain questions are fairly standard at interviews, eg good lessons and bad lessons, views on discipline, the role of the form tutor etc. An unsuccessful candidate most often hasn't prepared well for these questions and, as such, will have either glib or rambling answers. Use your notes to direct them as to what was a good answer and what was a bad answer to the questions set out for them in the interview.

Preparation of questions

Often candidates will ask silly questions for the sake of asking a question. It is important to emphasize that silly questions have the effect of undoing previous good work. It is also important to advise them on brevity. Pulling a list of 30 questions out of the inside pocket is not helpful.

Use your notes from the interview to recap on their questions and ask them to think about what sort of answers they were looking for and whether the information could have been gleaned from the information supplied to them either in writing or during the tour.

During the interview

How a person dresses, enters the room and their body language all have an effect on interviewers. From your recollection and notes, talk them through the process. What was your first impression? Shy? Nervous? Overconfident? Positive? Cocky?

Let the candidate know the golden rules (if they didn't come over well):

❑   Be positive.
❑   Smile.
❑   Have a firm handshake.
❑   Look people in the eye but don't stare them out!
❑   Try to build a rapport but don't treat the panel like old friends.

Body language

Body language during the Q + A session is also important. From the list below, select those that the candidate displayed and talk them through whether they are positive or negative attributes:

Positive

❏ Occasional affirmative nodding of the head
❏ Leaning slightly forward to show interest and engagement
❏ Sitting with hands, arms and feet unfolded
❏ Smiling where appropriate
❏ Sitting erect in the chair
❏ Firm handshake
❏ Appropriate dress
❏ Good eye contact

Negative

❏ Lack of facial expression, or an inappropriate expression
❏ Weak handshake
❏ Inappropriate dress
❏ Poor body posture
❏ Lack of eye contact
❏ Fidgeting or squirming in a seat
❏ Nervous habits or gestures
❏ Sitting with the arms, legs or feet folded

Answering questions

A common problem with candidates is not knowing how to answer a question. There are some good tips you can supply for those candidates who look good on paper but disappoint in the interview. Tell the candidates about what constitutes a strong answer:

❏ Back up a statement with a specific example (though not *ad nauseam*).
❏ Share the outcome or solution to a specific problem.
❏ Summarize to emphasize your strengths.
❏ Use active verbs.
❏ Use concrete examples.
❏ Be concise but complete.
❏ Be open.
❏ Be self-critical, but only when you feel confident that you can change.

Career development

Many candidates do not look beyond getting the job that they have applied for. Schools are not looking for people who want to coast or have an easy ride and get the job only to stay for the next 25 years with no thought to career development. A common interview question is about the candidate's aspirations. Many do not think ahead. You can advise candidates to think about their career progression:

❑ immediate career objectives (eg to gain experience and build on school-based experience for an NQT);
❑ medium-term career objectives (3–5 years): coordinator, head of subject, head of year etc;
❑ long-term objectives (5–10 years and beyond): middle management, senior management etc.

The important thing about a failed candidate's debrief is that it should be constructive and not demoralizing. If handled well, candidates should leave feeling that they have learnt from the experience and will be better prepared next time.

11

MANAGING CHANGE AND DEALING WITH CONFLICT

'Faced with a choice of either changing one's mind or proving there is no need to do so, almost everyone gets busy on the proof.'
John Kenneth Galbraith

Change is inevitable and today the pace of change in education is fast. No sooner do we seem to have implemented one set of changes than another set is winging its way to us from the DfES. Within schools there are many agents of change, from the governors to the headteacher, down the line to the new head of department. All will insist on changes and often the reasons for change are not made clear to teachers. For many, change is seen as a means to achieve progress; if we want to progress as a school and move up the league tables (often the one motivator that staff see as the cause of change) then new procedures, ideas etc have to be put in place. The person who carries most of the burden of change is the head of department, or subject leader – you. As the person who has to implement change, you are often in the unenviable position of having to introduce policies and procedures that may not have the full backing of all of your staff. Indeed there may be occasions when you personally will disagree with the policy or procedure.

FROM WHERE DOES CHANGE ORIGINATE?

Change can be imposed from above or demanded from below. Often the change from above will come from an interested party that is not directly involved in the school on a day-to-day basis, eg the DfEE or the LEA. For any change to be successfully implemented, a number of stages must be carefully navigated.

Moss Kanter (1984) describes two approaches to the introdu
products and technologies in the workplace: an *integrative* approach that
dealt with change across the workplace and a *segmentalist* approach where
change was compartmentalized. There are clear analogies within education,
with national initiatives such as the literacy and numeracy hour in primary
school and the key stage 3 strategy falling into the integrative category,
and a specification change for English, for example, being a segmentalist
type of change. Whichever type of change is needed, integrative or segmentalist, there are still some fundamental issues that need to be dealt with
and actions that are required for change to be successful.

Issues

❏ Understanding of how change is viewed and managed in the organiza-
    tion as a whole.
❏ The persuasion of staff of the need to invest time and resources in order
    to effect change.
❏ Problem-solving skills, team working and staff participation.

Actions

❏ A commitment from the senior management for the proposed change.
❏ Access to the appropriate bodies for support of the change (steering
    groups, governors, other middle managers, senior management teams).
❏ Wider lateral communication.
❏ Greater empowerment of staff, less hierarchical management.
❏ Wider communication of the need for change and how the change has
    been planned.

The starting point for any change must be a force field analysis to determine
the likelihood of success, followed by a needs analysis for that change.

FORCE FIELD ANALYSIS

Force field analysis is a method for listing, discussing, and dealing with
the forces that make possible or obstruct a change you want to make. The
forces that help you achieve the change are called driving forces, and the
forces that work against the change are called restraining forces. This

analysis helps generate options by examining the forces (groups, other activities, resources, relationships, etc) that can help achieve or work against the objectives.

Driving forces move the problem and the change in a positive direction towards solution and restraining forces move the problem and the change in a negative direction towards no solution.

Analysing these forces can determine if a solution can get needed support. In addition, it will identify obstacles to successful solutions, and suggest actions to reduce the strength of the obstacles.

The four-step force field analysis

Step 1 Produce a force field chart. Create two columns: one for driving forces and one for restraining.

Step 2 Brainstorm the driving and restraining forces (best done with the staff as a whole) and record them on the chart.

Step 3 Analyse the chart. Determine which factors can be altered to increase the chances of success.

Step 4 Decide if your solution is feasible. If it is, make a list of action items. If it is not, return to step 3.

If your force field analysis indicates that a feasible solution can be achieved, then move on to the needs analysis of change.

NEEDS ANALYSIS OF CHANGE

'If it ain't broke, don't fix it' is an all too common phrase and there is an element of truth within the phrase. But sometimes change is needed or even required, although what is to be changed isn't 'broke'. It is when this situation arises that you will find most resistance to change. In this case, as in all cases of change, you will need to carry out an analysis of change. The analysis will look at the motivation and need for change, the benefits and drawbacks of change, and the implications of change. Once the needs analysis has been carried out, a sensible plan for change can be drawn up and implemented. An approach to a needs analysis for change is given in Figure 11.1.

Once you have identified why change is necessary and what the benefits and incentives for change are, you need to examine the key relationships (see Figure 11.2) in order to assess the implications of change and arrive at a sensible implementation plan.

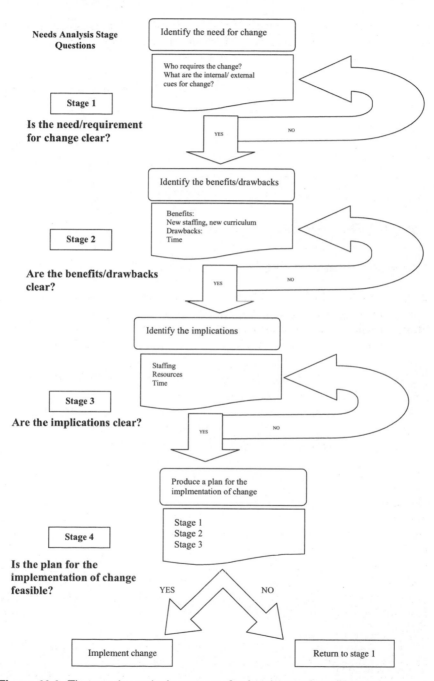

Figure 11.1 *The needs analysis process for implementing change*

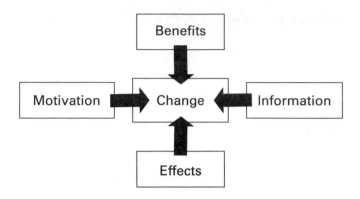

Figure 11.2 *The key relationships in change*

The motivation and need for change

What is the motivation behind the change? Until you have a clear picture of this, trying to implement the change in your department will be difficult. Understanding the motivation will allow you to reach logical, sensible decisions about how and when the change can be implemented and how successful it will be. The first thing to do is to identify who is requiring change and what their relationship is to the school, the pupils and staff. This is a simple matter in most instances and it does help the process to set out the interested parties and their motivation for implementing change.

Invariably there will be organizational cues for change. Your first priority is to decide what these are:

❑   falling examination results;
❑   low motivation (staff and students);
❑   poor attitude (staff and students);
❑   low expectations.

The agents for change will come either from within the organization or from outside agencies. From within, change may be instigated by the SMT, a new/existing head of department, the staff, pupils, parents etc. Agencies from outside may include the government, professional bodies, examination boards, consultants, OFSTED, industry, the community. Each of these agencies will have valid reasons for change. Not all of these reasons will be clear at first and it may require some research to find out why the change is necessary or in fact needed at all. In successfully implementing change, you must clarify the reasons for staff.

The benefits and drawbacks of change

Examine what opportunities or benefits exist should the proposed change take place:

❑ new staffing;
❑ new staffing structure;
❑ links to initiatives (local and/or national);
❑ new curriculum;
❑ improved results;
❑ improved attitudes and/or motivation;
❑ improved status.

The implications of change

❦ Any change, no matter how small, will have implications. They may be related to resources, funding, working procedures or working conditions. The relative importance of these implications will vary from staff member to staff member. As a manager, you need to assess the implications and their possible effects on the staffing, procedures and funding of your department or subject area. For those who have to implement and live with the change, the implications will be the most important aspect of change. It may have an effect on them that is either financial (an opportunity to gain promotion or take on paid responsibility) or affects their working conditions (more teaching, larger class sizes, extra work to familiarize themselves with a new specification etc).

For you there will be a different set of priorities, implications, benefits and drawbacks.

Planning for change

Any plan for change must have the following elements included if there is a chance for successful implementation.

Time

The time allocated for change to be effected may have an external time-scale (eg in 1995 we knew that the next curriculum change was due in 2000), or we may have an internal time-scale. This may require negotiation between the manager implementing the change and the agent for that change. What you believe is a perfectly sensible time-scale may not suit the agent for change. For example, staff may wish change now in order to effect an improvement in their working conditions, or the senior management may desire a change in the curriculum structure in the next academic year to alleviate staffing problems. You must decide on a sensible time-scale that accommodates the agencies for change and their time-scale. You must try in all cases not to agree to something so unrealistic or unachievable that any benefits of change are compromised. If you are pushed into a corner and 'forced' to agree an unrealistic time-scale then it is important that due consideration is given to this in the analysis of the implications and that these, wherever possible, are conveyed all concerned parties.

Resources

This must include physical as well as human resources. Any change will have an effect on resources and this, in turn, will have an effect on budgets. The effects on budgets may be directly costed to you as a manager (ie the extra cost of equipment, books etc will have to come from your capitation) or it may be a budget over which you have no control, ie a staffing budget or building or maintenance budget. The resources available can sometimes make or break any proposed changes.

Finance

Any proposed changes should be fully costed, both the costs that are attributable to you and your budget and the hidden costs. A failure to consider all costings when planning for change may mean that a lot of work put into the management of a significant change may be wasted. If someone whose budget you directly or indirectly call upon in order to facilitate the change blocks access to the funds, you may not be able to afford an aspect of your implementation. This may have a knock-on effect for the implications of change and therefore alters the nature of the change and how you proposed to achieve it.

RESISTANCE TO CHANGE

There are two main forms of resistance: systemic resistance, which is driven by cognitive factors, most often a lack of knowledge or a lack of skill, and behavioural resistance, when resistance can be due to a number of factors.

Systemic resistance

A basic lack of information may be put right simply by outlining the need for change and the benefits and incentives for change. A lack of skills will require more management, including support to acquire the skills and opportunities to develop new skills and update knowledge.

Where there is a lack of proper management there is also systemic resistance to change. When staff feel that change is inevitable and that the change is taking shape behind closed doors, there is a feeling that the 'management' are plotting. In truth it may be that the management are simply not placing an extra burden on the staff by doing much of the work to effect a change themselves. This can, however, backfire.

Behavioural resistance

Do not underestimate the perceptions that people will have about the proposed changes and how they perceive that change may affect them personally. People will also have set reactions to change, sometimes based on their beliefs, sometimes on their prejudices. People will also make assumptions as to why the change is happening and what the results of that change may be. Resistance to change will be greater if there is a lack of involvement in that change. This is characterized by 'The less I know the more suspicious I am' type of character and the more belligerent 'If I feel manipulated or shut out I will, no matter how good the idea is, be negative towards change'.

DIFFICULT SITUATIONS

As a subject leader or head of department you will encounter many difficult situations. These tend to be a result of attitudes and perceptions.

Attitude is the way you communicate your disposition to others and attitude is dynamic and sensitive and reactive to changes in the environment. Perception is the process of viewing and interpreting the environment (opportunities or threats).

Positive and negative attitudes

Positive attitudes result in seeing opportunities and setbacks cause you to rethink your attitude and see threats, not opportunities (ie negative). The trick is to shift people's perceptions to magnify the positive and diminish the threats. In shifting people's perceptions personality plays an important part. Personality is the mix of physical and mental characteristics of an individual. It is a product of our perception of others, and we transmit our personality. Others then interpret the messages and form a view of us. There are a number of factors that can influence or change a person's attitude. For example, a change in the environment (the work conditions), emotional events (either at work or at home), self-image (something that many actively seek to change), society's image – media representations, eg leather patches, mortar boards and chalk behind the ear. All of these may lead to conflict before, during or after change. The conflict may manifest itself in many different ways. Some strategies suggesting ways of dealing with conflict are described below, but it is important to note that your reaction and the reaction of others during periods of conflict will rarely fit a textbook description of a situation and that there is, correspondingly, rarely a textbook answer to resolving conflict.

Domination of a discussion

Try to use direct questions to others who may be present, and avoid looking at the dominant person when asking questions. You may have to chat privately to the dominant person.

Argumentative people

Revert to questions from an open forum, be direct and point out the time wasting that happens when an argument is carried on for argument's sake.

Antagonistic group members

Clarify the purpose of the meeting or discussion and offer them a free expression period. Try to discover their deep-rooted problems on a one-to-one basis.

Difficult subjects

Try to anticipate what the difficulties and objections will be. It may be possible to research feelings privately before the meeting or discussion. Be objective, but above all, remain neutral and do not promise what you cannot deliver.

MANAGING CONFLICT

Conflict can be constructive if handled carefully. You should encourage a diversity of viewpoints as this will, in turn, increase understanding of a position. Begin by asking the advocate of the conflict to articulate and support with evidence their objections to the change.

Assertive, yet negative people

When the issue is important, people can become quite assertive. This usually happens when they are confident in their knowledge and understanding. Sometimes it occurs when they feel that the discussion is 'going the wrong way'. Assertiveness can also be brought on when it is perceived that the opposition seems to have more power or influence than they do.

How do we make people cooperate?

People tend to cooperate when they:

❏ respect the opposition;
❏ value their relationship with the opposing person;
❏ recognize that something cannot occur without cooperation.

It is therefore important to clarify the objectives and to strive for under-standing. Make sure each party states their position with supporting reasons, but remember always to focus on the rational and to remove emotion and concentrate on facts and reasons. The key is to attack the problem and not the person. Personalizing an issue or resorting to personal attacks during conflict is immensely counter-productive. Try to generate alternatives and use others who are in the centre ground to formulate alternative actions. If possible, arrange a meeting or discussion and table the issue. Give the issue thinking time and adjourn to the next meeting.

12

LEGAL ASPECTS OF RUNNING A DEPARTMENT

*'A Schoolmaster should take such care of his boys as a
careful father would take of his boys.'
(Williams vs. Eady, 1893)*

The laws governing schools are many and varied. Many teachers think only about the laws that cover the information on pupils' progress that must be reported to a parent, or the requirement to deliver the National Curriculum. In reality there are many other statutes that may affect the teacher in the course of his or her work.

As a subject leader and head of department you must be a primary source of information for staff, though you are not expected to be a comprehensive legal guide and adviser. The following information has been summarized from a variety of sources, but principally from the Croner's Legal Guides (most headteachers subscribe to the *Legal Guide for Head Teachers*). Please note, however, that this chapter is not an exhaustive summary and you must have due regard to the *School Teachers' Pay and Conditions of Employment* currently in force as well as any local regulations as enforced by the LEA or employer.

For the purposes of this chapter the following broad areas will be considered:

1. Health and Safety at Work Act (1974)
2. Staff appointments
3. INSET
4. Financial management
5. The teacher's duty of care
6. Physical restraint of pupils

HEALTH AND SAFETY AT WORK ACT

This Act imposes a general duty of care on people associated with work activities. Its purpose is to reduce accidents and to improve health and safety at work. The administration of the Act is the job of the Health and Safety Commission (HSC) and its executive (HSE).

In essence the Act requires the employer to:

❏ have written policy statements and procedures for effecting the policy;
❏ make equipment and systems safe;
❏ make handling, transportation and storage of articles and substances safe;
❏ provide information, instruction, training and supervision to ensure H + S at work and access to them;
❏ provide a healthy and safe working environment and adequate welfare amenities, eg washing, toilets, heating, lighting and first aid;
❏ provide and maintain safe places of work.

In addition the Act requires all employees to:

❏ take reasonable care to avoid injury to themselves or to others;
❏ cooperate with employers and others in meeting their statutory requirements;
❏ not interfere with or misuse anything provided to protect their health, safety or welfare.

STAFF APPOINTMENTS

The Education (No. 2) Act of 1986 sets out the statutory framework for the appointment and dismissal of staff in county, controlled special agreement and maintained special schools. The LEA is required to set the complement of staff and is given general control of appointment and dismissal. However, under schemes of financial delegation (ie where the school has control of its budget) the governing body takes these decisions. Governors can expect to receive advice from their LEA and would also seek advice from the head.

Non-teaching staff

The governing body may recommend the appointment of non-teaching staff but must consult the head and, if the post is for more than 16 hours per week, the CEO of the LEA.

Qualified teachers

To teach in a state school you must normally have qualified teacher status (QTS) which is gained by completing an initial teacher training (ITT) course or programme. The minimum entry requirements for all ITT courses or programmes are at least a first degree (for PGCE or GTP) and the equivalent of a grade C in GCSE mathematics and English. If you wish to enter primary and Key Stage 2/3 ITT courses you will also need at least the equivalent of a grade C in a GCSE science subject (for those born on or after 1 September 1979). Although it is not mandatory, ITT providers are likely to require science GCSE (Grade C or above) for secondary courses as well. Please note that the above are minimum entry requirements and that ITT providers will have their own additional entry requirements.

There are three routes into teaching: undergraduate and postgraduate courses, employment based routes and flexible routes.

UNDERGRADUATE AND POSTGRADUATE COURSES

Undergraduate BA/BSc with QTS

With appropriate A levels (now AS and A2) and GCSE qualifications, it is possible to undertake a degree course that offers Qualified Teacher Status (QTS). There are a large variety of courses that offer QTS. They are normally four-year courses and comprise subject knowledge to degree level, school-based experience and the theories of teaching and learning.

Postgraduate Certificate of Education (PGCE)

Having completed a degree, there is the choice of a full-time one-year course leading to QTS, which combines subject and professional study with practical teaching experience. This is the most popular route into secondary teaching, although there are some places for the primary level. If you wish to extend your study over two years you can take the PGCE Part-time or if you wish to teach a different subject from the one of your current degree you may be able to take the PGCE Conversion.

In September 1999 the Government introduced a £5,000 financial incentive for graduates training as maths or science teachers. This was subsequently extended to all shortage subject teachers, increased to £6,000 and renamed a training salary. In addition, for those in shortage subject areas, such as science, maths, MFL and geography, an additional £4,000 was paid on successful completion of the induction year in a state-maintained school.

Flexible initial teacher training may lead to a PGCE and/or QTS. This allows career changes to remain in employment while they train as teachers with each trainees needs and circumstances looked at. The course is designed around an individual needs analysis and may last from as little as 12 weeks up to 2 years.

PGCE Conversion

This is a two-year course available for shortage subject areas at secondary level, currently including sciences, mathematics, design and technology, information technology and modern foreign languages. Although not compulsory, this course is generally advised if people wish to teach a different subject from the one of their degree.

School-Centred Initial Teacher Training (SCITT)

This is a scheme whereby you can gain QTS through training in a school setting. The course is a mix of theory and practice and includes a significant amount of classroom work. Courses last for one year and usually lead to a PGCE.

If a degree has not provided someone with sufficient subject knowledge to enter straight on to a one-year PGCE, you may be able to take a short bridging course. These courses are intended to help boost subject knowledge prior to beginning an ITT course. They are not intended to be an alternative to two-year PGCE Conversion courses, which cover subject study in much more detail. Bridging courses are available only in the secondary shortage subjects at present.

EMPLOYMENT-BASED ROUTES

Graduate and Registered Teacher Programmes

These programmes allow you to combine employment as a teacher with training leading to QTS. You need to be 24 or over and meet the minimum entry requirements for all ITT courses or programmes. You must first find employment in a school that is prepared to offer you training. For more information on these programmes, please contact the Graduate and Registered Teacher Programme Administration Unit. For more information on how these programmes operate in Wales, please contact the Welsh Office.

The Graduate Teacher Programme (GTP) is for graduates only. The programme will normally last a year. The degree should be relevant to the phase or subject you wish to teach.

The Registered Teacher Programme (RTP) is for those with two years' higher education. The programme will normally last two years. On the RTP you study for a degree at the same time as undertaking your teacher training, and QTS is only awarded when you have successfully completed both your degree studies and the teacher training.

The length of time the programme will last is flexible, depending on prior experience, but the minimum length of time for the GTP is three months, and for the RTP one year. It is possible to go on the programmes on a part-time basis but in that case training will take longer.

Overseas-trained teachers are eligible for either programme, depending on their qualifications.

You have to work at a school to go on the GTP or RTP, but it may be an ITT provider, LEA, employment agency or other body, which is responsible for planning and organizing your training. Your progress is monitored during your training and at the end of the training period an independent assessor assesses you.

A school may appoint a non-QTS graduate as an instructor provided there is no qualified teacher available.

Some people may train to teach in Further Education and may have an FETC (Further Education Teaching Certificate). They do not qualify for QTS, and neither does an HE trained lecturer who has obtained a University PGCTLHE (Post Graduate Certificate in Teaching and Learning in Higher Education).

It is worth noting here that the licence to teach, as it were, is the QTS, not a PGCE. It is entirely possible for a person to gain a PGCE but not have QTS. This would, in effect, place them on the non-qualified teacher's salary scale. The PGCE is an academic qualification awarded by an institution and is separate from the QTS, which is granted by the Secretary of State for Education and now governed by the General Teaching Council (GTC). Another anomaly occurs for those who fail their induction year. They may have a PGCE and also QTS, and neither can be taken away due to failure of an induction year, but their licence to teach in state and maintained schools will be revoked.

RESTRICTIONS TO EMPLOYMENT

Certain persons are not eligible for employment as a teacher, even though they may hold the appropriate qualifications. The Secretary of State for Education and Employment has the power to bar certain persons from employment as a teacher or employment in a school where close contact with minors (under 18s) is necessary.

Automatic barring

Automatic barring will occur for anyone who is convicted of or who has attempted the offence(s) of:

❑ rape or buggery;
❑ any sexual offence involving a child under 16 years of age;
❑ incest or unlawful sexual intercourse;
❑ indecent assault or gross indecency;
❑ taking or distributing indecent photographs.

Other cases likely to lead to barring

The Secretary of State also has the power to bar or restrict a person's employment for other kinds of misconduct, including behaviour which does not automatically result in a criminal conviction, including:

❑ violent behaviour towards children or any other offence of serious violence;
❑ a sexual, or otherwise inappropriate, relationship with a pupil, whether or not the pupil is over 16 years of age;
❑ a sexual offence against someone who is over 16 years of age;
❑ drug-related offences including trafficking;
❑ misappropriation of school property or monies;

❏ deception, eg misrepresentation of qualifications or failing to disclose past convictions;

❏ any conviction that results in a sentence of more than 12 months' imprisonment.

The police report to the DfEE all court convictions of teachers, youth workers or school ancillary workers except for minor road traffic offences.
Employers have a statutory duty to report all cases in which someone:

❏ is dismissed for misconduct;
❏ resigns after being accused of misconduct;
❏ resigns on the award of retirement benefits;
❏ resigns before enquiries into misconduct are completed.

(The above duty also applies to independent schools.)

List 99

Employers must check list 99, which contains details of people whose employment is either barred or restricted. Teachers included in list 99 are identified by name, date of birth and DfEE number (if appropriate).

References for department colleagues

From time to time you may be asked to write a reference or testimonial for a colleague or member of your department. In general terms, a reference is supplied in confidence to a prospective employer and is not usually shown to the person it applies to. Should you wish this absolutely to be the case, then you are advised to write 'In confidence' at the head of the reference. A testimonial or open reference may well be given to the person it concerns directly for their use. These are usually addressed 'To whom it may concern'.

Be advised that if, as a result of a 'bad' reference, a person fails to secure a post that they may otherwise have secured, you must be able to substantiate any claims made in the reference which may be considered adverse, eg bad time keeping, lack of class management skills, poor record keeping etc.

Trainee teachers

From time to time departments take trainee teachers from recognized ITT course institutions. A student teacher must be at least 18 years of age and have recognized entry qualifications for admission onto an approved course. The exact legal position of teachers whose lessons are being taken by a trainee are often a matter of concern – especially in practical subjects where there may be an extra duty of care with regard to Health and Safety. When a school accepts a trainee teacher, it must ensure that procedures are established that allow the student to develop professional skills but which places neither themselves, the pupils nor staff at risk. Effective supervision and guidance are, therefore, important. It is conceivable that if these were lacking and an accident occurred, the supervising teacher could be considered negligent by a court of law. For certain subjects, eg science, technology or sports subjects, supervisors of trainees should be especially careful. Trainee teachers may not have had a police check carried out before they are placed in schools. The DfES at present does not insist that police checks are carried out. Since trainees should be supervised, it is not deemed necessary. All trainees are asked to disclose any convictions and, should they disclose any conviction, then a police check is undertaken. Training institutions, however, cannot ask for checks to be carried out and invariably they apply to an LEA, which has the right to ask for checks, to check those who do disclose convictions. Many minor convictions do not warrant the trainee being barred from teaching, especially if they may have occurred in youth, such as shoplifting.

INSET

INSET should be linked with needs and be a part of all teachers' professional development. The extent to which various schools, departments and individuals plan and produce INSET will vary from school to school. As a general rule of thumb, an individual or department often bids for INSET. Participation should be voluntary and INSET activities should include:

❑ identification of needs;
❑ selection of priorities;
❑ implementation;
❑ evaluation;
❑ integration.

For INSET to be of benefit to the individual and/or department, it should meet the needs of the individual/department and not interfere with the day-to-day job of teaching but enhance that job. As a head of department you will need to identify the needs and priorities for your department and

135

plan a programme of INSET that will enhance both the teaching and the professional development of your staff.

With the advent of performance management, the issue of who is eligible and who should benefit from INSET is now more acute. In order to satisfy the threshold application, teachers must provide details of all relevant INSET and how it has helped them to perform better as a teacher. There is an implication for heads of department that they must, wherever possible and practical, assist staff in obtaining recent and relevant INSET. With INSET demands from all quarters of the school likely to exceed the budget available, the head of department will need to fight his or her corner to secure a fair share of the available funding. The funding is not just about paying for the course itself, there are also the knock-on implications of cover and supply teachers to be considered. The demands for INSET from staff must be balanced with a need to drive the department forward and also to provide continuing professional development (CPD) for the teacher. As a subject leader or head of department, your duty to your staff cannot exclusively be in relation to the performance of the department or subject; it must also be tempered with due regard for the performance of the individual.

FINANCIAL MANAGEMENT

LEAs are required to delegate the greater proportion of their expenditure on schools, including:

❑ the salary costs of teaching and non teaching staff;
❑ the day-to-day premises costs (eg repairs, decoration, rates etc);
❑ books, equipment and other goods and services (eg catering).

Heads of department are often given a delegated budget over which they have control regarding expenditure. That expenditure must be carefully monitored and heads of department may be required to account for their expenditure in detail. Part of the role of heads of department is to ensure that they are aware of their needs and prioritize their spending to meet those needs. Care should be taken in costing items for expenditure as overspending normally results in budget cuts in the following financial year. As a new head of department, a thorough audit of resources is often needed. This will identify areas of good, adequate and poor provision across a range of items from stationery to textbooks, consumables, audio-visual and computer equipment, and any specialist equipment. A review of allocation of resources is also needed to identify the level of spending required for each year group being taught, eg at the time of writing, the average cost of textbook provision per year for all subjects is £64 per pupil (years 7–11). This rises to £96 per pupil per year (years 12 and 13).

Financial management is often one of the trickiest areas of a subject leader's job. There is never enough money and no capitation allowance is ever adequate. The department may be a specialist one (eg art, design and technology, science) in which case the demands made on the school's budget can be quite large. Smaller, less demanding subject areas such as English or history, which do not have to rely on specialist equipment to deliver the National Curriculum, may feel that their allocation of capitation is less than fair. In all cases, demands for money must be rooted in a common sense approach to financial management. If your demands are excessive then the powers who have control of the purse strings will simply reject the demand and substitute what they feel is an appropriate amount. It is far better to negotiate a reasonable settlement, one that can be backed up with concrete evidence as to why this money should be spent, and set out a budget that you know the school can afford.

Schools must make their accounts known to interested parties. While it would not be proper for you to know the exact salaries paid to all staff, it is worth scrutinizing the yearly accounts to see where the money granted to the school is spent. It is not uncommon for 75–90 per cent of the budget to be spent on staffing. So out of a budget of, say, £2.7 million it is not unreasonable for £2.0–2.4 million to be spent on staffing. When your department or subject staff are demanding resources, appraising them of the whole school financial situation helps to put into context the demands you make of the senior management.

THE TEACHER'S DUTY OF CARE

Negligence

Negligence involves the breach of a duty of care owed to another person. If that person suffers injury or loss as a foreseeable consequence of a teacher's negligence, that person may claim compensation.

If negligence is alleged, a court will invariably ask two questions: 1) What (if any) duty of care was owed to the claimant, and 2) did the person against whom the claim is made fail to fulfil that duty – either by commission or omission? If negligence is proved, the court will then consider the following in order to assess the level of compensation: 1) to what extent the loss or injury is a direct and foreseeable result of the negligence, and 2) whether the claimant was partly to blame for the result (NB: very young or less able pupils are less likely to be considered to have contributed to the negligence).

The law decides on the *balance of probabilities*. This is not the same as the higher standard of proof required by criminal cases, which is *beyond all reasonable doubt*.

In the majority of negligence cases it is the employer who will be named and who bears responsibility. This may also be the case even if the teacher acts in a foolish manner or contrary to his or her employer's warnings/instructions. There are exceptions to this, but they are beyond the scope of this chapter.

In loco parentis

The classic definition of a teacher's general duty of care dates back to 1893. In a court case (Williams vs. Eady) the appeal court judge stated that a schoolmaster must 'take such care of his boys as a careful father would take of his boys'. This led to the concept of teachers being *in loco parentis*.

Delegation of duties by the head or other line manager

Where a headteacher or head of department delegates tasks to colleagues or to trainees under their care, they must be mindful of the principle of *delegatus non potest delegare*, ie the person charged with a duty cannot delegate responsibility for it to another, even though he or she may delegate the task itself. For example, if a class teacher asks a trainee to supervise the class alone, the teacher is answerable for that decision. If an accident occurs, a court would ask if the trainee had exercised proper care and whether the teacher who had responsibility for the class had acted reasonably in delegating control to that person. Negligence could be found in either case.

Care of pupils' property

Whenever a teacher takes charge of pupils' property, whether by request or by confiscation, they have a duty to take reasonable care of it. This may involve keeping it on one's person or locking it away in a room, cupboard, drawer, cabinet or safe. If a pupil suffers loss of property through negligence, he or she may claim compensation from the employer or the teacher, even if bringing the item to school is against school rules.

PHYSICAL RESTRAINT

Corporal punishment is a thing of the past. Violence towards teachers, however, seems to be on the increase. The number of cases of staff assaulted has risen and a recent court case upheld teachers' rights to refuse to teach a persistently unruly and disruptive pupil. This reasserted the right of teachers to teach and pupils to learn without fear of intimidation or threat of violence from a pupil. Teachers were given some control back when a new Statute upheld that teachers may use reasonable force to remove a disruptive child or prevent harm to themselves, a pupil or other pupils. As with all legislation, it is only going to be clearly defined once it has been tested in the courts. It hinges on the term 'reasonable': what, in the circumstances, is reasonable and what is not. There is no simple definition of what is and what is not reasonable.

In a situation where a six-foot, 15-stone teacher trained in martial arts puts a year 7 pupil into an arm lock, causing physical pain and muscle damage, a court would need to be satisfied that there was an imminent threat of serious injury to the teacher, the pupil or others. If that pupil were brandishing a knife, threatening another pupil, or had caused injury to another pupil, a court may rule that the teacher's action was reasonable and that his use of an arm lock to disarm the pupil was appropriate. If, however, the pupil had merely refused to hand over his comic, a court would rightly condemn that same action as unreasonable.

13

FINANCIAL MANAGEMENT

'Finance is the art of passing currency from
hand to hand until it finally disappears.'
Robert W Sarnoff

How the school is managed financially is ultimately the responsibility of the governors and the senior management team.

Many schools have developed systems for the distribution of monies within the school. Some schools work on an historic cost basis and the level of funding depends on the levels of funding given in previous years. Others use a formula system where the costs are calculated on a pupil-by-pupil basis, with a formula related to the number of pupils and number of pupil periods taught in any given curriculum area. Whatever system is in place, you must understand how that system works, both to your advantage and sometimes to your disadvantage. Whole school budgets are complex and different schools operate their budgets in different ways. Some finances are 'ring fenced', ie they are unable to be used for any other purpose than that specified by the people/organization that has allocated the funding. Other funding is more fluid and may be transferred from one budget heading to another.

Each year the governors must agree a budget for the coming year. For many schools this is simply an informative meeting where the head presents a budget that has previously been worked on by a governors' sub-committee on finance. The governing body will then agree the finance. Other schools may be in the difficult position of having a deficit in their funding. The problem here is that technically schools cannot set a budget deficit. Where the school deliberately overspends and is therefore 'in the red' they will find themselves in breach of DfES regulations. What actually happens in practice is that schools with a budget deficit must agree with the funding body (usually the LEA) on an action plan that will, in time, reduce the deficit and allow the school to operate. This cannot, however, be an open-ended plan and schools must strive to reduce or eliminate their deficit within, say, five years for a large (>£200K) deficit and in a shorter time for smaller deficits.

Some schools are in the lucky position of having a surplus. This can also cause problems, not least if staff grappling with out-of-date texts and equipment find that the school is sitting on a pile of cash. It is wise to be cautious, however, should you find that the school has a surplus. There may be very good reasons for having some surplus funds placed into a contingency fund to cover expensive and unexpected events, eg a replacement roof needed, structural changes as a result of new Health and Safety legislation etc. It has been known for some schools to accrue large surpluses (in excess of £0.5 million) which subsequently land the governors and management in hot water.

DEVELOPING GOOD FINANCIAL HABITS

Before you embark on a wish list of spending requirements, you need to do your homework to ensure that any requests you do make can in fact be seriously considered and not thrown out at the first stage:

❏ Get to know your school's budget and how it is operated and implemented.
❏ Schools have to publish their accounts and these should be available for you to peruse.
❏ Talk to the person delegated by the head to deal with financial matters (eg the school bursar or deputy head, or both!).
❏ Understand how the school is funded and look at the balance sheet.
❏ Talk to other heads of department about their funding and ask for their assessment of the system of allocations.
❏ In particular, talk to the heads of departments who have a strong practical element (eg technology, PE) to see how the school deals with capital purchases and maintenance.
❏ Conduct a through audit of your own department stock and equipment.

FINANCIAL SCHEDULING

You need to run your own budget alongside the school budget and you cannot easily therefore adopt a planning system that is out of step with the school system. If, for example, the school requires budgets to be spent by a

Figure 13.1 *Financial wheel*

certain point in the year, say the end of February, then there is no point arranging for stock or maintenance to be carried out and invoiced to you in March.

Once you know the system, and how it is operated, draw up a financial wheel that will allow you to plan ahead for income and expenditure (see Figure 13.1).

The wheel can be used to plot times when budget allocations are made, important dates for completing expenditure, and periods where ordering takes place and must be a priority for your attention. It will also allow you to keep track of budget meetings, not just those in which you are directly involved, but meetings between SMT and the governors and finance committees.

KEY FINANCIAL POINTS

There are two things that have a major impact on finance in schools: staff and pupils. This may seem like the obvious thing to state, but it is amazing how many of us forget this when asking for money or demanding increases in our limited budgets. If major savings in the budget have to be made, then the first thing to look at is waste, followed by cheaper goods. The last thing on a headteacher's mind is to save money by reducing staffing. This has a major impact on standards, results and probably more importantly on staff morale. From a subject head's point of view there should be no difference. The first way to make savings is to cut down on waste, followed by cheaper alternatives and, only as a last resort, a reduction in staffing.

When schools wish to increase their funding, their primary concern is to ensure that the school is full. If possible, schools will look to increasing pupil numbers in order to increase their overall funding. If you look at Tables 13.1–13.3, you will see the impact that staffing and pupil numbers have on the whole school budget.

Table 13.1 *Average secondary school pupil numbers*

YEAR	BOYS	GIRLS	TOTAL
7	75	83	158
8	61	87	148
9	78	71	149
10	70	71	141
11	46	40	86
12	61	69	130
13	5	15	20
Totals	396	436	832

Table 13.2 *SEN by stage*

	ASSESSMENT STAGE	PUPILS
1	Increased differentiation	36
2	Individual education plans	20
3	Involvement of outside agencies	10
4	Statutory assessments	2
5	Statements of SEN	6
	Total pupils stages 3–5	18

The tables give the picture of school funding and, although the figures will by now be out of date, the percentage calculations have not changed significantly in the intervening years. From this you will be able to see the general picture of funding and allocations in schools. It is easy to see that the number of pupils in any school has a significant effect on funding.

Table 13.3

BUDGET FORECAST

INCOME			
Income	Last Year '92 £	Forecast '93 £	Forecast '93 %
1. Basic Budget	0	£1,473,472.00	96.5
2. Additional SEN Funding	0	£7,488.00	0.5
3. Funding for minority ethnic pupils	0	£0.00	0.0
4. GEST or SPD(D)	0	£14,144.00	0.9
5. Other Grants	0	£7,488.00	0.5
6. Income from facilities and services	0	£21,632.00	1.4
7. Donations/private funds	0	£3,328.00	0.2
8. TOTAL INCOME	0	£1,527,552.00	100.0
9. INCOME PER PUPIL	0	£1,836.00	
Based on NOR	0	832	

INDICATIVE COSTS 1992/93

CATEGORY	£
Average secondary class teacher in the national system (with on-costs)	23,250
Newly qualified graduate teacher (with on-costs) 13,250	
Newly qualified certificated teacher (with on-costs)	11,750
Fully experienced without excellence points but five responsibility points (with on-costs)	27,500
Supply teachers – expected insurance bill for year – for whole school	1,300
Each member of educational support staff (for one full time equivalent)	9,000
Each member of admin/clerical staff (for one f.t.e.) 10,000	
Other supplies/services e.g. utilities (LEA estimate for whole school)	8,000
Buildings/grounds maintenance (LEA estimate for whole school)	7,000
Cleaning/caretaking (LEA estimate for whole school)	10,000

INCOME PER PUPIL	% of Total Income		
	Lower Quartile	Median	Upper Quartile
Basic Budget	92.5	94.8	96.7
Additional SEN funding	0.0	0.7	2.6
Funding – ethnic minority	0.0	0.0	0.0
GEST or SPG (D)	0.6	0.8	1.0
Other grants	0.0	0.4	1.2
Facilities/Services	0.6	1.3	2.4
Donations/Private Funds	0.0	0.1	0.8

EXPENDITURE PER PUPIL	% of Total Expenditure		
	Lower Quartile	Median	Upper Quartile
Staff			
Teachers	68.1	71.0	73.8
Supply/relief teachers	0.7	1.2	1.8
Education support staff	1.9	2.9	4.0
Admin/clerical staff	2.6	3.3	4.3
Other staff costs	0.7	1.0	1.5
Supplies and services			
Learning resources	4.4	5.4	6.5
Staff development/advice	0.6	0.8	1.1
Catering and other	1.2	1.9	3.0
Premises and special facilities			
Building/grounds improvement/maintenance	1.4	2.0	3.1
Cleaning and caretaking	3.0	3.6	4.3
Other occupancy costs	3.7	5.1	6.2
Special facilities	0.0	0.0	0.0

Excludes Middle Deemed Secondary Schools and schools with NOR<200
Note: Components of income and expenditure do not add to 100 in the table, reflecting the nature of median and quartile values.
Source of Data: Headteacher's Form. Acknowledgement with gratitude
Source of table – OFSTED

TABLE 5.6 SECONDARY SCHOOL CONTACT RATIOS 1995/96		CONTACT RATIO (%)		
Type of School	Number of Schools[2]	Lower Quartile	Median	Upper Quartile
Comprehensive	326	74.9	77.1	79.1
Grammar	22	74.8	76.8	77.6
Middle deemed Secondary	29	81.4	83.5	84.8
Modern	16	74.5	77.5	79.0
All Secondary Schools[3]	405	75.3	77.4	79.4

1. Ratio of number of teacher periods actually taught to total number of available teacher periods
2. Number of schools for which data are available.
3. Includes schools for which type is not defined.
4. Source of data: Headteacher's Form.
Acknowledgement: Source of table – OFSTED

TABLE 5.7 EDUCATIONAL SUPPORT STAFF IN SECONDARY SCHOOLS		JANUARY 1997	
Percentage of schools with			
Hours per 100 pupils	SEN Support Staff	Other Support Staff	All Educational Staff
0	22.2	0.2	0.1
0–10	41.4	3.0	1.2
10–20	23.2	40.2	17.4
20–30	7.6	43.2	35.4
30–40	3.3	10.3	24.7
40–50	1.3	1.9	11.6
All	100	100	100

NEGOTIATING WITH THE SMT

The principle of negotiation is a simple one. Successful negotiation means that in some way every party wins. The heads of department feel satisfied that they have at least part of what they want and the SMT feel that they have 'driven a hard bargain' for some form of return on their 'investment'.

How to conduct a successful negotiation

1. Develop a negotiation consciousness. Successful negotiators are assertive and challenge everything. In this context the word challenge means 'not taking everything at face value'. It means thinking for yourself. With a thorough knowledge of the financial system you will be fore-armed to challenge facts and figures given to you as reasons why something cannot be achieved or done.

2. Become a good listener. Good negotiators are good listeners; this allows you to ask probing questions. When you ask questions, wait for an answer. The person with whom you are negotiating will give up lots of information and you need to assimilate this.

3. Be prepared! Be a Boy Scout or a Girl Guide and never enter a negotiation 'on the hop'. Prepare your argument and bring with you any relevant data. If you are asked to enter a meeting unprepared, politely decline and offer an alternative. If you are forced into a meeting, make it clear that you are unprepared and cannot, therefore, make any decisions or agree to anything that is put to you until you have had a chance to look at the relevant information.

4. Aim high, but don't hit the roof. Your department will expect you to argue their case and to obtain 'the best deal'. It is wise to aim high but not to ask for the impossible. This is where knowledge of the school budget will be invaluable. If you can identify areas where there are potential savings, or if you can negotiate an increase in budget with a willingness to compromise elsewhere (eg on the photocopying bill), then you will more than likely be successful. If you ask for silly money you will almost certainly be rejected out of hand with no negotiation. Remember, sellers always ask for more than they can achieve and buyers always offer less than they are prepared to pay!

5. Be patient. Whoever is more flexible over time will win in the end. If the head is impatient for results and you can offer those results bundled with a package of finance to help you achieve them, then you are in the dominant position.

6. Focus on satisfaction. As a good negotiator you must help the other party to be satisfied. This means that their basic interests have been fulfilled. If the basic interest is results, then satisfaction will come when these are delivered. If you can promise this, given funding, then you are halfway to making the other party satisfied. Remember, however, you do need to deliver on your promises, so do be careful about what you promise.

7. Don't make the first move. Let the other parties make their demands first if at all possible. They may make demands that are not as bad as you imagined. If they are worse, you may have to adjust your strategy and refine what you ask for. If you have to make the first move, never open with what you will settle for after negotiation has ended.

8. Don't accept the first offer. If you do, this makes the other party feel that they could have got away with more. You must make a fight of it even if, as is sometimes the case, the offer is a *fait accompli*. You will also have to report back to staff, and the last thing they want to hear is that you capitulated on the first strike.

146

9. Don't make unilateral concessions. If you have to accept a decision then negotiate something in return. It is amazing how much more palatable a target or a cut is if there is something bright on the horizon, even if it is a simple gesture of new notice boards or a lick of paint over the summer!

10. Williams's Law. Always get it in writing! Always insist on recorded outcomes from negotiations. It is amazing how bad the memories of others are after they agree to one thing and then fail to deliver. If at all possible, get it in writing, or make sure that you record decisions, negotiations and outcomes as they happen. It is often a good idea to follow up a meeting that has not been minuted with a memo setting out what YOU think was said and agreed at the time.

However much money you have, it will never be enough, and however much money you ask for, you will never get it all, unless there are strings attached. When considering how much money is needed for your department you will need to consider a number of curriculum design factors. These factors (detailed in Table 13.4) will vary from school to school and by small amounts from year to year. All of the factors will have a bearing on how your budget should be allocated by the SMT, and when submitting budgets for consideration it is worth highlighting the demands made on your resources by the various factors. Some schools will have a system of formula funding and the person responsible for allocating budgets should explain how the formula takes into consideration the factors listed. Some of the elements listed in the table may be provided for centrally, such as examination entries, but who pays for the postage of coursework etc? Is this centrally funded or does the department pay? Sometimes items such this can prove a considerable cost to departments and many heads of department or subject leaders do not count these costs as an expense on their budget allocation.

Table 13.4 *Curriculum design factors*

FACTOR	
1	Cohort population
2	% of SEN pupils
3	% of high achievers
4	% of statemented pupils
5	Number of examination specifications
6	Number of examination entries
7	Breakdown of pupils per key stage
8	Number of lessons taught by key stage

CONSIDERATIONS WHEN CONSTRUCTING A BUDGET

Your priority when constructing a budget must be to ask the question, 'What will directly affect standards?' To find this out you may need to do a needs analysis to identify costs to the department. Begin by working out the cost of the following things on a pupil-by-pupil basis:

❏ stationery;
❏ textbooks;
❏ photocopyable resources;
❏ photocopying;
❏ consumables;
❏ ICT provision (hardware);
❏ ICT provision (software);
❏ capital equipment (overhead projectors, slide projectors, CD players/ cassette players etc).

Having assessed the costs, you will be able to see how much on a pupil-by-pupil basis you require in order to maintain the status quo. Any additional costs after this will be an enhancement to the provision. If your budget allocation allows for purchases, you may then consider what to purchase.

Before you think about making any purchases, apply the following criteria:

❏ Is the item matched to pupil needs and ease of teaching? If new equipment or resources are expensive, yet require particular expertise in order to use them, they will probably end up at the back of a cupboard, unused. Do the pupils really need this in order to learn more effectively and will teaching be more effective if enhanced by this new item?
❏ Is the item good value for money? Some items of software do not offer good value for money. They may look good and even sound good, but their educational value may be limited. This would not, therefore, be a value for money purchase.
❏ Is the item durable and appealing to pupils? What appeals to us as teachers does not always appeal to the pupils. If a new teaching aid is being considered, think about canvassing the views of the pupils on how they would like to see the item integrated into the day-to-day teaching.

Stock control is an essential part of the financial management duties of a head of department or subject leader. Are you seen as an easy touch by other departments for paper and exercise books? Do staff leave reams of paper lying about where pupils can just help themselves? Textbooks are always a problem and losing textbooks due to non-returns each year can incur a heavy financial burden on the department. Schools make a considerable investment in textbooks each year and a coordinated approach to their issue and return, and a school-wide policy on what steps to take to recover textbooks, is essential to avoid heavy losses. One strategy is to have all pupils sign for their textbooks (it's surprising how many claim they were never issued with one in the beginning) and to make it clear to parents that non-returns will be recovered by requesting payment. In one instance, a school employed a local firm of debt recovery agents to chase up non-payment for textbooks not returned. It was amazing how many parents and pupils suddenly found the missing books and returned them to avoid further letters. There is of course the danger of alienating parents with an approach such as this one, but the losses, when calculated by the school, amounted to over £8000 had the textbooks simply been replaced from school funds. Over 90 per cent of the money was recovered and the school did not have to resort to court action. Schools and departments have a duty of care towards the pupils, but they also have a duty of care towards the funds received and spent.

At some point there will be a call to cut costs. To cut any excess or wastage you must begin by cutting the waste first. One of the most expensive items in a department's budget is often the amount paid for photocopying. More often than not, the cause of excess photocopying is a lack of textbooks, combined with last-minute planning for lessons. If you look at the budget set aside for photocopying, it can be substantial. By analysing the type of copying and seeing how this could be reduced, savings can be made. Sometimes a commitment by the department to refrain from photocopying with the incentive of the purchase of new textbooks can still result in savings. Try to produce filed banks of worksheets and encourage staff to build them up slowly, not carry on repeating orders for 30+ copies simply because you cannot find the last lot. At times when change necessitates extra financial commitment, you must build in start-up costs to the change and request an exceptional payment or grant from the school's reserve in order to effect the changeover.

Another source of funding is local (sometimes national) business. If there are local businesses who are refurbishing or refitting, some items may be of considerable use, though do beware of the implications of taking second-hand electrical goods (including computers) and ensure that they are properly tested and safe to use. Look out for opportunities to bid for monies from within the school (eg the Parent Teacher Association) and from outside (eg charitable organizations).

APPENDIX A

THE ATTITUDE SURVEY INTERPRETATION SHEET

The attitude survey is not a test of competence in a job; it is merely a summary of the environment in which you work. As with all tests of attitude, only the person who fills in the questionnaire can judge how truthfully they have answered. The results may be influenced by certain conditions, eg how easy/difficult a day you have had, how things are at home, whether you feel well or unwell, whether you have recently applied for a job and been successful or unsuccessful. The results of the survey are for you to know only, and no names are attached to the survey.

Interpreting your score

The scoring sheet has interpreted your responses to give a rating to *your* job under the following headings:

1 ACH = Achievement
2 RY   = Responsibility
3 RN   = Recognition
4 AD   = Advancement
5 WI   = Work interest
6 PG   = Personal growth

It is important to note that the assessment is not of *you* but of the extent to which you feel that your job contributes to each of the above areas. These areas or headings are those that are widely regarded as 'motivators' in the workplace. If you add all of the scores together you will get a grand total which will determine overall job satisfaction.

Some general interpretations

If you look at your score in relation to the UK and European norm, you will get an indication of how your job satisfaction compares.

	ACH	RY	RN	AD	WI	PG	Overall
UK and European norm	3.1	3.0	2.9	3.2	3.6	3.5	51.8

As a rule of thumb, a score of 3.5 or above in any of the areas indicates job satisfaction. A score of between 2.5 and 3.0 suggests that there may be room for enrichment of your job. If you have a score of below 2.5 in any area then you need to ask yourself why. It may be that there is a simple reason. If you were to ask the headteacher about opportunities for further advancement it may result in a very low score. This would not mean that the job is not satisfying.

If you look at the overall score, then a score of 55 and above indicates complete satisfaction with the job. However, there is a relatively wide margin here and anything between 45 and 55 would not/should not be a cause for concern.

When deciding what to do about areas where there is a low satisfaction score, it is important to look at who is empowered to change or improve the job. For the first three areas, your line manager may well hold the key to improved job satisfaction.

Should you decide to survey your colleagues, please ensure that they are made aware of its purpose and its limitations. It can, however, be a good starting point to discussing their job satisfaction. After all, if they are happy in their work, it can only make your job easier and more satisfying!

APPENDIX B

Time log

Name:		Department:	
Week beginning:		Day:	

Basic statistics			
Number of contact hours allocated per week (h:m)		Number of taught groups allocated	
Number of non-contact hours allocated per week (h:m)		Number of pupils allocated	
Amount of designated meeting time per week			

Teaching	Prescribed	Administrative	Planning	Marking	Discretionary
T	P	A	Pl	M	D

Task	Designation code	Brief description	Time taken (mins)

CALCULATIONS

For each designated activity, work out the percentage of your working day associated with each category and add this to the summary sheet.

Summary log

Name:		Department:	

Total number of allocated teaching groups = _____

Total number of pupils in allocated groups = _____

Total number of hours worked during week (TN) = _____ (round to the nearest half hour)

Actual number of contact hours (T) = _____ % contact time = $\dfrac{T \times 100}{TN}$ = _____

Actual amount of prescribed time (P) = _____ % prescribed time = $\dfrac{P \times 100}{TN}$ = _____

Actual amount of administrative time (A) = _____ % administrative time = $\dfrac{A \times 100}{TN}$ = _____

Actual amount of planning time (Pl) = _____ % planning time = $\dfrac{Pl \times 100}{TN}$ = _____

Actual amount of marking time (M) = _____ % marking time = $\dfrac{M \times 100}{TN}$ = _____

Actual amount of discretionary time (D) = _____ % discretionary time = $\dfrac{D \times 100}{TN}$ = _____

For ease, this information may then be displayed as a bar chart or pie chart to help you visualize exactly where time is being consumed. It is odds on that the amount of planning will go down as the amount of administration and discretionary time increases!

Remember to include evenings, Saturdays and Sundays in your log of work.

REFERENCES AND BIBLIOGRAPHY

REFERENCES AND GENERAL READING FOR CHAPTER 1

References

Blake, R and Mouton, J (1964) *The Managerial Grid*, Gulf Publishing
Department for Education and Employment (DfEE) (1998) Teachers: meeting the challenge of change, Government Green Paper, DfEE
Everard and Morris (1996) *Effective School Management*, 3rd edn, Paul Chapman Publishing
Fayol, H (1949) *General and Industrial Management*, Pitman
Gray, H (1984) *Contributions No. 6*, Centre for the Study of Comprehensive Schools, Nene College, Northampton
Taylor, F W (1911) *The Principles of Scientific Management*, Harper & Bros.
Tannenbaum, R and Schmidt, W (1958) How to choose a leadership pattern, *Harvard Business Review*, March/April
West-Burnham, J (1997) *Managing Quality in Schools*, 2nd edn, Pitman Publishing

General reading

Barker, A (2000) *How to be Better at Managing People*, Kogan Page
Bennett, N (1995) *Managing Professional Teachers*, Paul Chapman Publishing
Kemp, R and Nathan, M (1989) *Middle Management in Schools: A Survival Guide*, Simon and Schuster Education
Buckby, R (1997) *Management in Education*, December
Bush, T and West-Burnham J (1994) *Principles of Education Management*, Longman

REFERENCES AND GENERAL READING FOR CHAPTER 2

References

Bennett (1995) *Managing Professional Teachers*, Paul Chapman Publishing
Cole, G A (1996) *Management Theory and Practice*, Letts
DfEE (1998) Teachers: meeting the challenge of change, Government Green Paper, DfEE

General reading

Angus, L (1993) The sociology of school effectiveness, *British Journal of Sociology of Education*, **14** (3), pp 333–45
Dunham, J (1995) *Developing Effective School Management*, Routledge

REFERENCES AND GENERAL READING FOR CHAPTER 3

References

DfEE (1998) Circular 2/98: Reducing the Bureaucratic Burden on Teachers, DfEE
Davidson, J (1999) *The Complete Idiot's Guide to Managing Your Time*, 2nd edn, Alpha Books
Heslop, N, Brodie, D and Williams, J (2000) Hodder Science Series (Hodder and Stoughton) associated Web site at www.hodderscience.co.uk

General reading

Blair, G M (1999) *Starting To Manage: Essential Skills*, Chartwell-Bratt
Busher, H (1988) Reducing role overload for a head of department: a rationale for fostering staff development, *School Organisation*, **8** (1), pp 99–103
Earley, P and Fletcher-Campbell, F (1989) *The time to manage: department and faculty heads at work*, NFER/Routledge

REFERENCES AND GENERAL READING FOR CHAPTER 4

References

DfEE (1999) *The Standards Site: Action Plans* (www.standards.dfee.gov.uk/ guidance/action/index)

Poster, C and Poster, D (1993) Headteacher appraisal, Chapter 15 in *Managing the Effective School*, ed M Preedy, Open University

General reading

Clift, P *et al* (1987) *Studies in School Self Evaluation*, Falmer Press

Fullan, M (1988) Change processes in secondary schools at the local level, *The Elementary School Journal*, **85** (3), pp 391–421

Fullan, M (1991) *The New Meaning of Educational Change*, Cassell

Mortimore, P *et al* (1988) *School Matters*, Open Books

Van Velzen, W *et al* (1985) *Making School Improvement Work*, ACCO, Leuven

REFERENCES AND GENERAL READING FOR CHAPTER 5

References

Adair, J (1986) *Effective Teambuilding*, Gower

Belbin, R M (1981) *Management Teams – Why they succeed or Fail*, Butterworth Heinemann

Cole, G A (1996) *Management Theory and Practice*, Letts

Curtis, S and Curtis, B (1997) *Managing People and Activities*, Pitman Publishing

Maslow, A (1987) *Motivation and Personality*, 3rd edn, Harper and Row

Tuckman, B (1965) Developmental sequences in small groups, *Psychological Bulletin*, **63**, pp 384–99

General reading

Bell, L (1992) *Managing Teams in Secondary Schools*, Routledge

REFERENCES AND GENERAL READING FOR CHAPTER 6

References

Barker, A (2000) *How to be better at. . . Managing People*, Kogan Page
Decker, B (1988) *How to Communicate Effectively*, Kogan Page

REFERENCES AND GENERAL READING FOR CHAPTER 7

References

Campbell, J and Neill, S R St J (1997) Managing teachers' time under systematic reform, Chapter 7 in *Managing People in Education*, ed T Bush and D Middlewood, Paul Chapman Publishing

REFERENCES AND GENERAL READING FOR CHAPTER 8

References

Fletcher, S (2000) *Mentoring in Schools: A Handbook of Good Practice*, Kogan Page

General reading

Russell, T (1996) The role of school managers in monitoring and evaluating the work of a school: inspectors' judgements and schools' responses, *School Organisation*, **16** (3), pp 325–40
Vann, B (1996) Mentoring Middle Managers in a Secondary School, *University of Leicester, Continuing Professional Development News*, Summer

REFERENCES AND GENERAL READING FOR CHAPTER 9

General reading

Ribbins, P (1985) The role of a middle manager, in *Managing Education*, ed M Hughes, P Ribbins and H Thomas, Cassell, London

Metcalfe, C K (1985) Appraising appraisal: an examination of some of the issues involved in staff appraisal in secondary schools, *British Journal of In-Service Education*, **11** (2), pp 91–95

Metcalfe, C K and Russell, S (1996) 'I didn't trust them but they were nice': the link between inspection and school improvement, *Journal of Teacher Development*, February, pp 44–50

Trethowan, D (1987) *Appraisal and Target Setting: a handbook for teacher development*, Harper and Row, London

Brydson, P (1983) *Heads of Department and self evaluation*, University of Hull

Bullock, A (1988) *Meeting Teachers' Management Needs*, Peter Francis

REFERENCES AND GENERAL READING FOR CHAPTER 10

General reading

Carlson, R (1971) Effect of interview information in altering valid impressions, *Journal of Applied Psychology*, **55** (1), pp 66–72

Funder, D C (1987) Errors and mistakes, *Psychological Review*, **101**, pp 75–90

Hinton, P R (1993) *The Psychology of Interpersonal Perception*, Routledge

McCleary, L and Ogawa, R (1989) The assessment centre process for selecting school leaders, *School Organisation*, **9** (1), pp 103–13

O'Neill, J, Middlewood, D and Glover, D (1994) *Managing Human Resources in Schools and Colleges*, Longman

Parker-Jenkins, M (1994) Part time staff recruitment: an equal opportunities dilemma, *Management in Education*, **8** (2), pp 3–4

Riches, C (1992) Developing communication skills, in *Managing Change in Education*, ed N Bennet, M Crawford and C Riches, Open University Press

REFERENCES AND GENERAL READING FOR CHAPTER 11

Reference

Moss Kanter, R (1984) *The Change Masters – Corporate Enterprise at Work*, Allen and Unwin

General reading

Dalin, P and Rolff, H-G (1993) *Changing the School Culture*, Cassell

Dimmock, C (1995) Restructuring for school effectiveness, *Educational Management and Administration*, **23**, pp 5–18

Earley, P (1990) Piggy in the middle: middle management in education, *Education*, **176** (10), pp 192–93

Fielding, M (1996) The muddle in the middle, *School Management Update*, *TES*, 19 January, p 8.

Harrison, B, Dobell, T and Higgins, C (1995) Managing to make things happen: critical issues in team management, in *Vision and Values in Managing Education: Successful Leadership Principles and Practice*, ed J Bell and B Harrison, David Fulton

Jenkins, H (1991) *Getting it Right, A Handbook for Successful School Leadership*, Blackwell, Oxford

Schein, E (1980) *Organisational Psychology*, Prentice-Hall

Stephenson, T (1985) *Management, A Political Activity*, Macmillan

Yeomans, R (1987) Leading the team, belonging to the group, in *Readings in Primary School Management*, ed G Southworth, Falmer Press

REFERENCES AND GENERAL READING FOR CHAPTER 12

General reading

Croner (2001) *The Legal Guide for Headteachers*, Croner Publications

Croner (2001) *Manual for Heads of Science*, Croner Publications

Croner (2001) *The Teacher's Legal Guide*, Croner Publications

Croner (2001) *Teachers' Rights, Duties and Responsibilities*, 4th edn, Croner
    Publications
Croner (2001) *A–Z Guide to Education Management*, Croner Publications

REFERENCES AND GENERAL READING FOR CHAPTER 13

General reading

Croner (2001) *Financial Management for Schools*, Croner Publications
Downes, P (1991) Costing the curriculum, *Managing Schools Today*, **1** (3), pp
    20–21

INDEX

Adair, J 24, 51
academic achievement 48
achievement 62
activity log 30, 152–54
action plans 41–49
  characteristics of 41
  evaluation of 42, 48–49
  implementation of 42
  inspections and 41
  monitoring 48–49
  planning cycle 42
  prioritization 43–46
  review of 42, 48–49
  target setting 43–46
Adams, D 29
administration 30, 80
advanced skills teachers (ASTs) 4, 6
advancement 62
advertisements for staff 110
agenda *see* meetings, agenda for appraisal 4,
  35, 44, 61
attitude survey 13–16, 150–51
authority 8, 25, 84
  defined 26
automatic barring (from employment) 133

Belbin, RM 58, 60
Bennett, N 18
Blake, R 10, 22
Brodie, D 38
Brunel university viii
budgets 140, 141, 143–45
  constructing 148–49
burdens (on teachers) 33

Campbell, J 79
change 118–19

actions 119
  agents of 122
  benefits of 123
  drawbacks of 123
  implications of 123
  integrative approach to 119
  motivation for 122
  needs analysis of 120–22
  planning for 123
  resistance to 124
    behavioural 124–25
    systemic 124–25
  segmentalist approach to 119
clerical work 80
Cole, GA 21, 22, 51, 70
committee 58
communication 66
  behavioural skills 67–68
    dress and appearance 68
    eye communication 67
    gestures and facial movements 67
    humour 68
    language and pauses 68
    listener involvement 68
    natural behaviour 68
    posture and movement 67
    voice and vocal variety 68
  effective 66–78, 92
  interpersonal 67–69
  media 72–74
  networks 70–72
    all channel 70–71
    chain 70–71
    circle 70–71
    wheel 70–71
    Y 70–71
  obstacles 76–78

of meaning   66
organizational   69–70
overload   77–78
communication skills   ix–x, 31, 38, 66–78
confiscation   138
conflict   x, 84–85
escalation of   84
managing   127
ways to avoid   84
consultations   39
continuing professional development
   (CPD)   34, 136
criminal convictions   111
Curtis, B   54
Curtis, S   54

Darwin, C   46
Davidson, J   29
decision making   23, 25–28
and consultation   26
scientific approach   25, 26
styles   26, 27
process of   26–27
ten-step process of   27–28
Decker, B   68
delegation   34, 72
of tasks   34, 55
of duties   138
of responsibility   138
department   21, 128
legal aspects to running of   128–39
deputy heads   17, 70
development plan   43, 48, 70
DfES (DfEE) (DES)   4, 6, 17, 33, 39, 41, 42, 96,
   118, 133
circulars   78
Standards and Effectiveness Unit   41
discipline   93
dissatisfaction   63
Drucker, P   8
duty of care   xi, 128, 137–38
   in loco parentis   138
   negligence   137

e-mail   72, 73
education act   129
employment, restrictions to   133–34
automatic barring   133

failing staff   86, 103
Fayol, H   7
finance   124, 128
financial management   136–37, 140–49

and curriculum design   147
financial habits   141
financial points   142
financial scheduling   141–42
formula system   140
historic cost basis   140
Fletcher, S   86
flexibility   85
force field analysis   119–20
driving forces   119, 120
four-step approach   120
restraining forces   119, 120
funding, local and national   149

goodwill   85
governors, school   43, 44, 70, 73, 74, 103, 118,
   140
graduate teacher programme (GTP)   131–32
Gray, H   3
Green Paper (on education)   4, 17
groups   51, 53
effective characteristics   52
ineffective characteristics   52

head of department   vii, 6, 24, 25, 95, 98, 101,
   102, 118, 136
head of science   26
heads of year   53
headteachers   vi, vii, 44, 54, 70, 118
health and safety (act)   128, 129
employee's responsibilities   129
employer's responsibilities   129
health and safety commission (HSC)   129
health and safety executive   (HSE)   129
Hertzberg   vi, 62, 63
hygiene-motivation theory   vi, 62–63
Heslop, N   39
hygiene-motivation theory *see* Hertzberg

inspection   4, 5
influence   25, 84
defined   26
initial teacher training   130–31
inset   viii, 34, 55, 79, 128, 135–36
Internet   38, 39
interpersonal relations   62
interview debrief   114–17
interview procedure   107–12
information to candidates   110
candidate selection   111
case study analysis   113
in-tray exercises   112
interview   111

role play 113
psychometric testing 113
    ability and aptitude tests 113
    personality measures 113–14
interviews, staff 105, 111, 129
  group discussion 112
  halo effect 105
  inappropriate questions 106
  leading questions 105
  listening during 106
  note taking 106, 112
  panels 105, 111, 112

jargon, use of 77
job description 35, 108

LEA 43, 44, 118, 129, 130, 136
leader 18, 57,
  appointed 21, 25
  charismatic 22
  functional 21, 24
  situational 21
  subject 21
  traditional 21
  with vision 19
leadership 4, 17–28, 57
  authoritarian 22–23
  democratic 22–23
  effective 18
  good xi
  group vi, 6
  in schools 17
  inappropriate styles of 23, 24
  individual 21
  ineffective 18
  of teams 17
  operational 21
  strategic 21
  styles 22–24
  types of 20, 21
  variables affecting 22
league tables 96
legal aspects 128–39
list 99 134
LMS 2, 5

management v, 1, 3, 6, 12
  and leadership 17–18
  classroom 2
  crisis 32
  defined 7
  driving force for 3
  effective v, 16, 32

four spheres of 1, 8–10
  determining 8
  measuring 9, 10
  organizing 9, 10
  planning 9, 10
ineffectual 12
lack of 125
of change 4, 118–27
of conflict 127
of schools v, 4, 33
of staff performance x, 4, 96–103
problems 12
relationship-orientated 23
'scientific' 7
structure 10, 17
styles viii, ix, 10–13, 17
task-orientated 23
theory 1, 8
training in schools 3–4
manager 2, 3, 57
  defined 2
  departmental 4
  line manager 39–40
  natural managers 19
marking 30, 79, 93
Maslow, A 62
Maslow's hierarchy of needs 62
McGregor, J 51, 64
media 38
meetings x, 30, 32, 40
  agenda for 80
  attendance 81
  debate during 83
  departmental 79
  ending 81
  management of 79–85
  middle management 41
  minutes of 81
  moaning sessions, avoidance of 82–83
  outcomes of 80
  senior management 41
memos 40, 72
mentor 86–95
  choice of 89
  listening skills 92
  mentee relationships 87
  sharing expertise 91
mentoring 86–95
  communication in 91
  expectations 89
  nature of 90
  stages in 87
    communication 88

fulfilment 88
  introduction 87
  redefining 89
underperformance 93–94
middle manager vii, 25, 33, 37–38, 44, 54
minutes *see* meetings, minutes of
misinterpretation 66
misunderstanding 66
moderating 79
Moss-Kanter, R 119
motivation 60–63, 64
Mouton, J 10, 22

national college for leadership (NCL) vii
national curriculum 4, 5, 46, 137
national professional qualification for
  headteachers (NPQH) vii
national standards for subject leadership vii
Neill, SR St J 79
negotiation 145–47
newly appointed staff 86
newly qualified teachers (NQTs) 86, 90, 91,
  112, 117
  induction 112
non-teaching staff 95

objective setting, performance management
  101–02
observation
  during performance management 100
  of lessons 92
  of other teachers 102
OFSTED viii, 42, 93, 110, 122
organization
  of people 7
  of work 7
overseas trained teachers 132

parent teacher association 149
parents 36–37, 43, 74
part-time staff 86
pay deal (Scotland) vi
performance management *see also* managing
  staff performance 96–103
  philosophy for 97–98
  roles and responsibilities 103
  setting objectives 102
  threshold 97
performance management cycle 98–103
  stages of 98–101
    monitoring 100
    planning 98–99
    review 100–01

performance management policy 98
performance review 100–01
person specification 108, 109
physical restraint (of pupils) 139
PIA triangle 27
policies, school 21, 39, 53, 62, 70, 93, 118, 129
post graduate certificate
  conversion (subjects) 131
  in education (PGCE) 130–31
  in teaching and learning in higher
    education (PGCTLHE) 132
Poster, C 44
Poster, D 44
power 25, 84
  defined 26
presentation skills 74–75
procedures, school 21, 39, 53, 70, 118, 129
professional development objectives 102
pupil progress 101
pupils 36–37, 38, 43, 46–47, 61, 71, 101
  physical restraint of 128, 139
  property 138

qualifications and curriculum authority
  (QCA) 38
qualified teacher status (QTS) 130, 131, 132

race relations (act) 111
recognition 62
Reddin's 3-D theory 23, 24
references, supply of 134
registered teacher programme (RTP) 131–32
rehabilitation of offenders (act) 111
relationships 10, 11
report writing for projects 73–74
resources 54, 124
  books and equipment 136
responsibility 62
results 10, 11
  comparison of 37–38

salary 62, 136
schemes of work 38–39, 53
Schmidt, W 10, 11, 22
school
  culture 32
  day 29
  organisation 32
  policies 21, 32, 39
  procedures 32, 39
  promotion in vi
  timetabler 25
school centred initial teacher training

(SCITT) 131
school funding 143–45
second in department (2iC) 83
senior management team (SMT) 37, 54, 70,
     74, 84, 94, 122, 140, 145
  negotiating with 145–47
senior teachers 17
set lists 33
sex discrimination (act) 111
situations, dealing with difficult 125
  antagonistic people 126
  argumentative people 126
  assertive people 127
  difficult subjects 126
  domination of discussion 126
  negative attitudes 125–26
  positive attitudes 125–26
solutions, proposing 84
special educational needs co-ordinator
     (SENCO) 72
staff 128
  appointments 129
  dismissal 129
  interviews 104–10
  searching for 104
  selection 104–17
stock control 148
student teachers 134
  supervision of 135
subject leader 98, 101, 102, 118
super-heads 23–24

Tannenbaum, R 10, 11, 22
target setting 45, 48
  stepped targets 45
Taylor, FW 7
teacher training agency (TTA) vii, viii
teacher's pay and conditions x
team building 50–65
  constraints 53
  stages 54–58
    forming 56
    norming 57
    performing 57
    storming 56
team leader 53, 57, 98, 99, 101
  role of in performance management 99, 101
teams 19, 35
  commitment 26
  concept of 54
  defined 51
  effort 19
  growth 56
  motivation 60

responsibilities 55
roles 55, 58
  chairman 58
  company worker 59
  completer 60
  innovator 58
  monitor 59
  resource instigator 59
  shaper 58
  team worker 59
  success of 55
teamwork 51
telephone conversations 73
textbooks 39
theory X 64–65
theory Y 64–65
time 123
  administrative 30, 31
  contact 29, 31
  non-contact 29, 30, 31
  prescribed 30
  teaching 31
time management ix, 29–40, 93
time wasters 31–40
trainee teachers 61, 80, 86, 90, 134–35

undergraduate courses (for QTS) 130
underperformance, staff 93–94
  stances taken 94

vision 17, 54, 70
  communication of 17–18

Wall Street v
Wallace, AR 46
Web sites 39
Weber, M 8
West-Burnham, J 12
Woodhead, C 93
World Wide Web (WWW) 72, 78
  misinformation 78
workers 20
working conditions 28, 62
working environment 29
working party 58
working week 30, 79
Williams, JD 39
Williams's law 147

X theory *see* theory X

Y theory *see* theory Y

Zander, B 50